£4

Poetry Ireland REVIEW 95

Eagarthóir/Editor

EILÉAN NÍ CHUILLEANÁIN

© Poetry Ireland Ltd 2008

Poetry Ireland Ltd/Éigse Éireann Teo gratefully acknowledges the assistance of The Arts Council/An Chomhairle Ealaíon and the Arts Council of Northern Ireland.

Poetry Ireland invites individuals and commercial organisations to become Friends of Poetry Ireland. For more details please contact:

Poetry Ireland Friends Scheme
Poetry Ireland
2 Proud's Lane
off St Stephen's Green
Dublin 2
Ireland

or telephone +353 1 4789974; e-mail management@poetryireland.ie

PATRONS:
Joan and Joe McBreen   ColourBooks Ltd

ISBN: 1-902121-33-3
ISSN: 0332-2998

ASSISTANT EDITOR: Paul Lenehan, with the assistance of Lucile Dumont, Amélie Covo and David Maybury

DESIGN: Alastair Keady (**www.hexhibit.com**)
Printed in Ireland by **ColourBooks Ltd** Baldoyle Industrial Estate Dublin 13

Contents

Poetry Ireland REVIEW 95

Angela Long

TOURIST

Like a hungry tick,
I root for pulse points,
along the fissure of a grike,
the translucence
of a harebell's neck.

I bite where the membrane is thinnest,
where the blood runs hottest.

You extract me whole,
but I am lodged here,
festering,
blooming red rings
around my point of entry.

Michael McCarthy

THE MORNING BOBBY KENNEDY DIED

The Dalmatics, red, gold, purple, off white
have been allocated in pairs. Steve and I
get the green ones. Eamonn and Billy
are in red. Dr Seeldrayers is giving the organ
full throttle as we process in. The ceremony
lasts two hours, and when we come back out
it's done. We're in it now for the long haul.
Next year will be Ordination proper.

Mc Mahon with the rust coloured hair
is at the door offering congratulations.
'Allow me Mick.' 'You're allowed.'
A few of the boys have lit up with relief.
I'm smiling in the afterglow of it.
The organ has followed us outside
mixing in with the smell of laburnum
and cut grass. The sky is overcast.
Someone says Bobby Kennedy is dead.
I didn't even know he'd been shot.

Michael McCarthy

BELOW THE WELL

Mushrooms grow wild in the round field,
they hide in the dewy grass, their heads bald.

You can pick a few and bring them home,
as many in your hands as there is room.

Don't put them in your pocket, you'll forget
and they'll only get bruised and break.

Peel them, lay them on the range, let them sit.
Watch their pink ridges darken and go flat.

When they start to sizzle put them on a plate,
sprinkle them with salt, cool them with your breath,

Lift them up with a fork, don't spill the juice.
Shape your lips like you were giving a kiss.

They'll be like the host on your tongue only hot
and they won't stick to the roof of your mouth.

Alan Jude Moore

MRS COLOHAN

I am piecing together a map
of unknown relatives
and others encountered
when I could not tell
what they might have meant to me
or I to them

except hands held briefly
and dark smiles in hospital yards
half stolen from photographs
ushered back into the car
down long driveways home

filing sweets and change
by weight in suitable pockets

           ★

I am piecing the map together
the good and the bad
to fill the gaps left
by language bitterness and death
stretched by silence

I am not sure what you can tell me
I am almost unknown
and getting older

           ★

I will pinpoint past lines drawn
across the city like a latticed tart
again and again
back and forth

we have fallen in
risen up and out of it
laid down beneath
this heap of red brick and gougers

often I felt it would collapse
or melt into the silt
and say we never existed
without this

two strands connected
where water meets the road
and you might have considered
men across the river
asking questions of engines
and the mechanics of trade

waiting boats and motorcars
bicycles and trams

to be bought or to be sold
honesty / dishonesty

the stinging grease and frying fat
speckled counter in Gloucester Street

wounded hands salted
and out into the night-town

these are the beginnings
the formation scars

waves well before breaking

stone steps to the river

Toon Tellegen

'MY FATHER...'

My father
choked on his daily bread
and on his millions of debtors

wherever he went
my brothers crackled under his feet,
wherever he slept
forgiveness dangled gently in the wind

he kissed my mother
              in the shadow of the hereafter,
fumbling with the angry buttons of her soul,
and my mother exclaimed:
'what are you doing? why are you kissing me?
why don't you give me a kingdom? now and here!
oh please...!'

but my father said amen,
he gave nothing,
he is one of us.

                    – translated by **Judith Wilkinson**

Toon Tellegen

'MY FATHER...'

My father
stayed out of the picture

it was summer,
my mother was being demolished,
my brothers broken down one by one

the sun was shining
and life became somehow unpleasant
and unmistakeably unspeakable–
no one knew what was the use of other people,
passers-by dragged superfluous love along

dust clouds lifted
and a house was built
made up of one maddening mother
       and indeterminate brothers in abundance

and on the rocks,
     lean and lost sight of,
my father
who stayed out of the picture.

– translated by Judith Wilkinson

Simon Ó Faoláin

SOS COGAIDH

Léim anuas ded' chapaillín spágach *piebald*,
tar i leith gan néall buille ná luan amhrais id' thimpeall
agus bainfeadsa clogad mo chlaontachta díom.

Nach cuimhin leat mé, a fhir theann dhuibh,
nó an bhfuil an sciamh chéanna orainn uilig id' shúilibh?
Ar imeall Chill Mocheallóg tharraingis scian orm.

Is cé gur ormsa a bhi do bhior dírithe
bhi sé ar nós nár fhaca tú éinne,
bhi sé ar nós gur throidis le scátha.

Is cé gur agatsa 'bhí greim ar an chos,
do bhraitheas mar lia ag faire frithluail,
toisc scian do leigheas ar gach aicíd dod' chás.

Níl fonn orm riamh toil dheona a cheilt
ach ní féidir linn cumhacht seanthaithí a shéanadh,
'cuireann uisce le fiacla chon agus dhuine.

'Gus an gcloífidh an beirt againn galar seo *Pavlov*,
chun go gcífear an duine taobh thiar den aghaidh fidil
gan néall, gan luan, gan clogad ná scian?

– Buaiteoir, Duais Cholm Cille, Féile Idirnáisiúnta Filíochta Bhéal Átha na mBuillí, 2008

Tom Mac Intyre

IN AND OUT OF HER DREAM

We're in one bed, that atself, only a country
road's the bedroom. This tramp, Arab
complexion, shows. I pour him whiskey,
lots. Gulp, gone. Next that *Tigress & Cub*

out of all the Blake etchings. And thrawn,
spectre thrawn, her cheek beside me. 'Don't
stir,' I whisper. They leave us well alone.
Now I regale her with a childhood dunt,
slán beo happy ever rafters, someone

else's dowry, not mine: from an upstairs
window I fire an orchid, bold arc
of my covenant, to the Protestant *Denise*,
blonde shimmer below. The street empties.
'So what's that about?' O, mighty ask!
We know, sortov, *The Search* is dour work,

rejoice in holy sweat. She's a blue-blood
of Florentine stock, it's fifteen somethin',
Savonarola toast, Ficino Platonic aubade.
'What's,' steadying a huff, 'it all mean?'
More wine, I suggest. She gives the nod,
Chianti a must. Chocolate the vine,
the Tuscan drumlins, our country road,

chocolate the tramp's bowling silhouette,
'My orchid flung to the Planter belle,'
I say, 'it's all in that striped vignette,
wish I could revisit your dream, enable
flight of that cojones flower, contest
schismy quiet of the purged street, *Terrible*,
I wrote once, *terrible how empty a street
can be...*' Quoting oneself is truly sinful.

Away into herself she goes, away, away...

Richard W Halperin

OF COURSE YOU

Of course you dreamed me. First, the top
Of the hill, the grass, the scorched path,
The yellow sun. Then, an old man
Descending, carefully, on a pony.
A knock on the wall, hard – are we
In a room? whose? – and Shelley is drowning
In the lake. The smell of the hill,
The tufts of parched grass, the wind ruffling
The pony's mane, the veined hands
Of the old man, not attending to the pony,
A girl child leading them, so gently.
Had there really been all that pain?
Had it really been worth it? And
There is Shelley engrossed, lying on
His stomach in the grass by the shore,
Reading some tract or other; so, that,
Or the other, was a rumour.
Then, the sun (it was noon) slid down
The cheek of the sky like a teardrop.
It was hard to believe that that
Could make the bright blue bluer, but it did.
You had always known, to comfort
Was at the heart of love. But for some of us,
The knowledge takes longer.

Mary Rose Callan

FINE DAY

Early afternoon in the brand new
extension, a final
                    touch

of paint. You lean
                    into an alcove
above the cooker, white-

coated like gloss you're applying,
almost disappearing,

thin, tall, in your prime.

I offer words about this fine
day, half-hearted, spattering
                          silent

brushstrokes, over-shoulder smile.
Before another
                full day
                        passes,

hurrying to meet a friend,
your breath, your heart's beat

all at once
            ceases

in a future we can't imagine in this
room, a new space of lost light

reclaimed from the garden.

Kevin Kiely

SOLUBLE ASPIRIN AS REVELATION

Outside –
human sized trees
phantasmagoric figures
snowcapped
as if lurching through the slant blizzard

limbs and wands raised, half-mantled, gleaming
on the topside of branches

sky: an ocean of frozen silver
hedges & bushes bobbed in snowfur

avians on dawn patrol, flit, fly, gone
to the unheard music
of frostlike sugar, sweet and looking salty

this toothache awaits the transcendent
blizzard in water with effusion of jet engines

across a rainy sky, the nibbled half-moon tablets
through falling snowflakes
rising in a tidal wave

oscillating out of orbit inside the glass tumbler
scintillating distant stars to ease the pain.

Susan Rich

ENTERING THE ABANDONED RED BARN, OLD PHOTOGRAPH

A periwinkle glimpse of sky, a pliant web
of walking and corn silk revealed

as we make our way, honeycombed together,
revised by October stems and leaves;

satisfied with a walking stick, a condom,
and two mugs of cinnamon tea;

certain no one else had ever done what we would do –
create languorous love against

abandoned stacks of hay and watch
as the New England shifting clouds repeat,

repeat, repeat their message
love me, leave me, love me

as the dogs, Sasha and Sarajevo tongue
my palms, protest his ridiculously cunning knees.

And afterwards, after Sunday morning
news, and afternoon raspberry creams –

we wave goodbye – backpacks packed
thumbs angled out against the sky.

And I listen for the skeletal recalling
of our muscles, cartilage, and limbs;

yes, regrets, yes,
in louder, less extinguishable cries.

Pauline Gillan

WHO CARES?

Who cares that I grew up
A thousand miles away,
In a woman's house,
Two miles outside the town.

Uncles came round twice a year,
And looked us up and down.
We did not look like starving,
My mother and I.

While China cups were laid
And the Simnel cake brought out,
They talked about each other, also
My mother and I.

They seemed surprised each year
That I had grown an inch or two,
What else could I do? It was all very polite,
And they went home before it was night.

Patrick Carrington

WITH MY HANDS I REMEMBER

I wander room to room on quiet nights
when sleep is too bitter
and touch what you touched,
take from books and boxes your hand,
from oil smudges your scent,
from darkness light that like the sun
is nowhere to be found. I kneel

in sand at dawn and place my palms
in footprints to turn your toes
around. In morning fog
a shape on the dunes could be
anything, but I paint you. I walk

to breakfast and remember how you loved
only the purest things. And I trace,
on a dusty plate of your china,
the honest circle of you. I too now love
that red ring, the soft touch
of brush to bone with a simple curve.

Ted Deppe

UNDER THE HOSPITAL MOON

Four a.m., my wife awaits emergency surgery,
I'm camped by her bed, listening to her dream
or hallucination about Fred Astaire and Ginger Rogers,
when her roommate calls from behind the curtain:
Are you two awake? Talk loud enough I can hear you.

Bette's been through everything Annie's facing
but her voice is still bright: *How do you like this Pleur-evac
that drains my chest tubes? It makes a racket
but its rhythm's sort of calming.*
I tell her it sounds like the white-noise machine

we bought when we moved back from Ireland:
I thought the suburbs would be quiet! And Annie,
my medicated darling, says, *All those face-lifted homes
need an army of leaf blowers and pool cleaners. Right?
All those face-lifted, tummy-tucked, liposuctioned homes...*

Down the ward, someone's in crisis, Dr Blue is paged,
footsteps and carts rush past and we pause to listen,
then Bette says, *God bless somebody. And you think
the suburbs are noisy! You should have heard
the car alarm in the parking lot last night:*

like a bleeping space ship crashing into a fireworks factory.
I try to listen past her, to what's happening down hall,
but Bette's caught the same wave as my wife: *That alarm
was so awful it was almost funny. It made one noise
like a police car rolling off a pier, backwards.*

*But in the end, I sort of liked it. It just sang
like a catbird drunk on berries under the hospital moon.*
Like the one sober guest at a party of the muses
all I can do is hold Annie's hand and smile
as Bette jokes quietly for a few minutes more,

words like small, worn coins, like white noise,
or drops of morphine, till Annie sleeps again.
Bette's quiet now, too, so I give myself to the rise and fall
of the Pleur-evac, which almost covers the three of us
with the sound of waves, or breathing.

Kristiina Ehin

'GOOD FORTUNE MY APPLE-CHEEKED SISTER...'

Good fortune my apple-cheeked sister
is wiping dust off the sewing machine
She has black hair and
a cruel gaze

Peace my tempestuous brother
rampaged the shadows into a muddle today
He arrived from Easter Island
a bunch of dried tree roots outstretched in his hand
the darkness of the sun bulging in his bag
hormones scratching his throat
in his blood the joy of triumph
that buried
intimations of twilight

I am a tsunami
that leaves
your boat untouched
I overturn big ships
batter beach hotels to bits
soak wedding photo albums through
carry kittens far out to the open sea
tear wild boar skins from hunting lodge walls
and dance with dead butterflies and children's prams
towards the cold
rising of the sun

I am a man who knew the speech of cats
now I have even forgotten the mice
and dice
I crawl like a rat into a hole
and like a mole close the mouth
When you come
I bow down deep
into myself
You won't have noticed
the dust of love in my eyes

Spring evenings still cool
tracks unnoticed
doors unlocked
Still
I leave with the clamour of the fair in my ears
pain hammering in my heart

The land – that softest of
cutting boards –
carries me
again into evening
In the crumbled bones of gravel paths
in the blood-red bright shadow
of peony bushes
I fall asleep before the TV of the sky
neither happy nor at peace

Mrs sun rises
first in the morning
I right behind her
We heat up the satellite dishes
unlock
office doors and mouths
I and the sun
apologise before all the world's offended
drive couples together again
and speed shyly
and passionately beside each other
towards the years of wearying
towards the dross of feeling
I and the sun
set alight the new-moon half
And nod off pounding
The last tower bells against the abyss

I and the sun
from a tribe of cremators
float downstream
together with lavish maiden-wreaths

– translated by **Ilmar Lehtpere**

Peter Bakowski

ADOZINDO FERNANDES AND HIS FAMILY OF OLD MACAU

The mending of nets,
the scrubbing of decks
for a plug of tobacco,
a bucket of fish-heads,
a few silver coins,
each long day
except Sunday and feast days.

Evenings are ours,
to sit to food,
father's questions,
sometimes barbed as fish-hooks,
sometimes doing the work of the sickle, clearing weeds
that threaten the proper growth of a crop.

Father releases me from the table and house
and I stroll
the cross and bend of streets
to buy
a mango, a watermelon, a salted codfish
or nothing,
content to hear
a bird twittering
in its cage on a first floor balcony.

The pulling down of shopfront shutters,
the undisputed meandering of stray dogs
tell me it's late.
I return to our street,
its steep ascent
a challenge now for grandpa.
I slump onto a chair,
reach for a drinking glass, the pitcher of water,
open the windows
to the gift of a breeze.

All around the sitting room walls
hang framed photos of cousins, uncles, aunts, great grandparents.
Shopkeepers, civil servants, soldiers and engineers,
In Mozambique, Goa, the Azores and Macau.
Some never left their small village in Portugal.

The one who never married,
the one who kept a mistress,
the one buried with honours,
the one buried in a pauper's grave.

The one who died in childbirth,
the one who became a painter,
the one who told fortunes,
the one who left behind
a scandalous diary.

Photos of those we knew,
photos of those we never knew,
whose stories are changed, dramatised
in the retelling.

The family blood in our veins,
the signature that must be my own.

On the roof of the grain store,
the weather vane turns.
A burdened donkey labours up the hill.

Alan Kellermann

THE GREY HOUSE, 1917*

Cattle skulls hang, threatening rain, over my return
to the city of my sins – the city I belong to but will
never inhabit. My children raised it from
mud and dry straw in porticos and parapets –
a dome boasting to dead sky.

                             I still remember
the first brick – the cornerstone in thirty years
of walls. That's the way it is with brick: one
upon another until you can't see the living
for the dead; a border you don't realise
until it's finished.

                     And always, the falcon –
hung-head and talons scritching like untended
toenails – hooking the dull cut of his mad
basalt eyes over our shoulders while we raise
his people's walls in stout brick. Houses
rising over our own built from memories
and reminiscences we stack together like sticks
singing
         we shall rise again
                                 to drown out
the rumble of history collapsing around us, tribes
divided by walls we've made – not at the end
of the lash, but from fear, only, of what leaving
means.

        I still keep a tunic by the door. Its perfect
white linen reminds me of water – I was pulled
from water they say – the spray at the crest
tears loose, arcs clean and falls. Here
there's only sand swallowing the bodies
we don't have time to bury. The dead
root us an inch deeper every year, and mothers
thread their resilience into baskets for fresh reeds.

The Grey House (1917), oil on canvas, Marc Chagall

Michael Heffernan

PURPLE

I may need to recall the given year
this happened, if it's different than I thought.
All I need to do is sit back on the chair
I have beside the old table I bought,
and look up at the ceiling with my hands
hanging down loosely backward, as at ease
as I can be in the sharp part of my brains
where I keep most of my liveliest ideas,
sometimes before I even put them down,
and often without ever doing that,
so I take one of them and look at it –
in this case it's the one about my death
and whether there had been a sliver of sun
on the purple wall. And I take a breath.

David McLoghlin

IN THE UNDERGROUND CAR PARK
  – for Katie Armstrong

In the underground car park
of the mortuary chapel
the brothers in their black suits are gathering round.
Narcotic fumes hang in the air.
Car doors slam.
The coffin slips in.

'I suppose they'll go slowly,'
someone says.

They'll go slowly through Dublin
until they reach the road to the west
then they'll go like the clappers
to Sligo
through the streaming rain
following their mother home.

Ainín Ní Bhroin

I COULDN'T FIND THE MARAIS DISTRICT

The following morning
I told him I wanted to be on my own
for a couple of days.

I walked along Rue de Clichy
near the Moulin Rouge.
It was all porno shops.

An Algerian man
tried to hold my hand.

I was thinking about
a photograph of us
where I was leaning
on Yeats's headstone.
I was wearing a grey cardigan
and grey trousers.
He didn't like jeans.
The photograph
made me look happy.

I got to the Place de la Bastille
and looked in the windows
of the furniture shops.

I ordered monkfish
in a small restaurant.
Its flesh was the same colour
as the tips of his ears.

Gare du Nord
was filthy.
Abbesses too.

I put my carnet
under the strap
of my watch.

Colette Connor

I remember you standing by the window:
'These days we don't think of anything much.'
In the blue of your eye that looked heavenward,
Disappointment clung to the iris like a shroud.

I could see that you had given in:
You tried so many times to right yourself.
One day you gave it up, packed it in:
'I'll never worry about that again.'

From that day onwards, I watched your decline:
How you stopped noticing the world around you.
Refused to answer the knock at the door,
Stood staring out the window at the sky.

And no one knows who or what maimed your heart,
No, no one knows who or what, only I.

Martin Bennett

'A long time in the city pent' and then,
the other end of the line, we step down:
Whoosh! All's limitless azure and oxygen –

past roof or turret of small Renaissance town
sea's abstract fresco stretching the eye's reach,
distance turned ultimate decoration.

Across a meadow, on the adjacent beach
yesterday's secretary or pedant now leap,
now loll under the first serious sun

this year, carefree flesh awaiting its Matisse,
somewhere the same's spirit blithely sketching,
each glint his glasses taking it all in.

Gráinne Tobin

SCABIES, 1970

The whole town knew someone in the prison –
pinpoints of blood on the children's sheets
were not from hives or the strawberry harvest.

Our mother, mortified!

My new English boyfriend
on his first visit home to meet my family
shared the jar of petrol emulsion
we brush-stroked on each other's seamless bodies,
interning the mites that burrowed under warm skin,
suffocating their insurgent itch,
sealing their tunnels with poisoned residue.

His scarified torso, the unclean stigmata
we couldn't explain to his parents.

Old sores on both our houses.

Michael Coady

THE JOIE DE VIVRE OF ANNICK AND PIERRE
  – *for Paul Durcan, Paris, April 2008*

Bonjour Annick et Pierre
je suis Irlandais,
a stranger, chancing by today
out of all the catchment of our lives

and tributary streams of happenstance
it took to carry each of you, and me,
to this, your delta place –

just across the path from where
in Cimetière Montmartre
Vaslav Nijinsky is slouched in bronze
over his own grave,
downcast as Petrushka,
immortal puppet yearning always
for a human heart and face.

Nearby, a woman on a bench in April sunshine
turns her head to see
whose photograph I'm taking,
then continues on imperiously
filing her nails, while from another
corner of her eye she oversees
her man, who's within range
and hunting down someone's last earthly
resting place, as I

point the lens to find and photograph
the street snapshot of Annick and Pierre
that someone singled out
in truth and love and grief
to set in stone
between their names and dates.

So there we meet for the first time,
although they can't see me
within their moment's frame. I see
a man and woman, young but not
too young, sure of each other, smiling,
in some time and place, some why and where,
open to whatever's on the way,
walking hand in hand down a bright street
that leads them on towards eternity

flourishing in their free hands
ice-creams (*cornets à deux boules*)
that they're about to eat.

What are your choice of flavours
on the day
Annick and Pierre?

Fruit de la passion,
menthe chocolat,
pomme verte
or *jasmin,*

pétale de rose,
vanille
or *caramel,*
framboise or *fraise?*

It lifts my heart to meet you on this day,
Annick and Pierre,
the pair of you
still showing all the living and the dead
how to be human in this world,

hand in hand
and walking with your ice-creams,
down some street and round a corner,
radiant and brave,
and just about to taste.

Gabriel Rosenstock

HAIKU

baby frog!
who was
your mother

where is
she now

this autumn day

HAIGA ARTWORK BY Ion Codrescu

Pat Boran

PROVISIONAL

When a youngster dies,
the whole town comes to a halt.
They cry in the street,
in the corner shop,
at the till in the supermarket,
they cry holding hands at school.
They cry who have felt
death move among them,
rattling the pens in a pencil case,
turning the pages of a textbook
with his icy breath.

How else could it be
in a town so small
the priest plays golf with the father,
the gaunt gravedigger
is the mother's second cousin (once removed),
and his lock-jawed son –
the first on the scene, as it happens –
only two years before
himself almost perished
on this same stretch of road
they shuffle up now,

dust in their faces,
the wind whipping around them,
sending their hats into orbit
like souls that swoop and swerve
always out of reach.

Pat Boran

Dream of the Sparrow Morning:
a line from some imagined Chinese poem,

or a fragment of wisdom,
blurred by translation,

or something glanced at, flicked through
in a bookshop somewhere
years ago,

and forgotten
until now,

the line Dream of the Sparrow Morning
comes back to you,
comes back *for* you,

wakes just before you do
in the dawn light,
to whisper in your ear.

And the more you think on it,
puzzle over it,
the more the phrase
professes no great
interest in meaning.

Dream of the Sparrow Morning:
5 words finding each other,
like a burst of colour on a hillside field,
the wild-flowers of language.

And yet, now, watch as they lend themselves,
title-like, to everything you see:

your shirt and jeans draped over the chair,
your shoes standing by to useless attention,
your curled up wristwatch on the bedside-table,
foetal, like you, and blank in the grainy light.

Dream of the Sparrow: Morning.

Dream of the Sparrow-Morning.

Or, my favourite interpretation,
Dream of the Sparrow (comma) Morning.
An exhortation. A prayer of breath.
A call for this bright morning to produce
that plump brown-grey short-tailed bird
whom Sappho imagined
drawing Aphrodite's chariot
through the heavens.

Dream of the Sparrow, Morning:
the soft landing of that comma
perfect somehow (the happy accident
of its worm-like appearence)
as you draw back the curtains to reveal
the lawn outside and find
the sparrows have indeed arrived
before you, have settled, all business,
dreamt up by morning, conjured by it,
and making the most of the light.

Macdara Woods

SONG

Air: 'Dicey Reilly', slowly

Rose from my bed to mend my head
And fumbled out the door
Into the street to find relief
As many times before
With one sleeve on and one shoe off
Astray in time direction lost
And the start of my ruin was rising early

Still searching for the Angel
I went walking through despair
And when we met she told me
That I lived in disrepair
It's clear said she you're sorely pressed
Out here again and half undressed
Oh the start of my ruin was rising early

I thought that life was love revealed
That everyone agreed
That no one there intended harm
Kind lilies of the field
Beneath my feet no stones of doubt
Until the tide of youth went out
When the start of my ruin was rising early

I learned the cost of what I'd lost
But learning comes too late
So little time for love or rhyme
With the Piper at the Gate
To wreak in full the banishment
Of all who don't put by the rent
And the start of my ruin was rising early

And thus the years have come undone
To leave me walking still
Along the docks and promenades
In the morning river chill
There's no going back I must go on
Each night and day pass through the dawn
For the start of my ruin was rising early

Jason Gray

BEAR

Along the trail, I drag my shadow behind me
As the sun burns into my forehead. The woods
Of Virginia do not move, except everywhere,
Slowly. Ahead, the stillness is the same.
Even the trees are bending with the weight
Of air. I've walked for miles and yet seen nothing.
No scurryings, only wind-howls at cliff-edges,
Where stunted pines like suicides look down.

Down into the valley, the light dulls.
What's left luminous is the moss in shadow.
And in the river basin, among the deadfall,
Scruff sparks in the brush and out comes a bear,
Running into the woods. I stand amazed.
Like darkness exposed to sunlight. An empty bowl
To water. The footbeats leave their echoes.

Damian Smyth

THE COONEYITES AT COOLACREASE

"There was some trouble about a pathway last year, but this was settled long ago,
the path having been given to those who claimed a passage through it."
    – Miss Pearson, Coolacrease, Co Offaly, July 1921

I

It is the job of the stranger in a place to be hospitable,
to have his sojourn through a lifetime uneventful; to be wise;
to keep himself to himself, but not so much to seem offhand or odd;
to find ways always, even when most unlikely, to give way.
So, after the killings – the bleeding to death in the farmyard
bothering the livestock, cigarettes nipped off in the flowerbeds –
they were right, of course, those that were left, to make little of it
and it was anyway true that their peculiar behaviour
(no papers, no radio, no telephone, spare words in the post),
meant their news was slow and discreet even among their own,
such as they were. For Scripture is clear and needs no gossiping.
They had always been hunted, they'd told themselves, from the
    catacombs,
although we know they have no pedigree whatsoever,
and can be traced no further back than to a few headcases
ranting as usual and gathering adherents only decades ago,
for all their self-regard, for all their secrets and meetings in their houses,
their big fat fields, their itinerant preachers so oddly well off.
It wouldn't have occurred to themselves, of course, the Cooneyites
of Coolacrease or Ballywarren, those hostile townlands,
that they weren't Christian at all; but Magi, pagan, aloof and
    deserving all they got.

II

It may be time to visit those farmsteads in County Down,
the austere and governed, the efficient and unremarkable,
the escaped, the dug into the landscape, the invisible
outposts of the Cooneyites among the lax orthodoxies around.
How they came to their encampments, the Two-By-Twos, footwear
    shaken
at every milestone, prosperity and family forsaken

in favour of the enigmatic God of a few stray passages
vigorously read, exhaustively understood, pursued and executed,
to settle like tinkers or old sailors or mad soldiery
so off the beaten track, so far inland, so wounded,
is less interesting than the simple fact they did;
found something at a distance from others and themselves
which bound them quickly and fast to those they had commerce with
and in this place particularly, where faith and its law part company.
An outlaw life – poverty, vagrant action, attack –
dead by settlement, marriage, tillage and sweat,
a different irruption, a melancholy and mellower love,
if it wasn't that each July, in a pond on their own land,
they dip themselves without reserve under the surface
of everything the complacent, ordinary universe holds true.

III

At a certain point, isn't it true that going to the water
in that way, in public, is an exposure so intimate it's like flowers
are falling off the shoulders accidentally bare,
like white flowers caught in the tight tresses of the knotted hair
or across the wide chests of farming men suddenly vulnerable?
That is the miracle. Behind the counter of that small shop back then,
you raise your eyes to what is no more than a silver bracelet of skin
showing above sensible boots and the great skirt a girl has already
   thrown
over the whole world to shade it from a light too bright to bear
and, in the doorway, in their scrubbed hands the exact change ready
   made,
tall hats, bonnets, cummerbunds, an ulster buttoned tight against
   the wind.
There is war in the world but the incognito heart survives
the trench, the camps, the bombs, the two towers kneeling down
and the recurring armistice of every compromise to keep the peace.
It's beautiful. And different. And no less safe. And dangerous.
Now it's a throwback, regressive, rural and oddly pastoral,
at odds with iPods and MP3s, the whole shebang of SMS,
these genteel roundheads digging in their heels, saying nothing,
arguing nothing, online nowhere, but somehow so persuasive
   children stay
and eventually draw their dowdy suitors in to the sober coupling of
   mallards.

IV

It is the simplest thing in the world to kill a man,
paying no heed to prattlers on the struggles of conscience
or the practical considerations which come into play.
It's a matter of settling that it must be done. After that,
it's routine, more or less professional, and thrilling,
going through whole lifetimes in an afternoon, a house left
burnt and ruinous, strung out in a meadow like a line of wagons.
The photographs afterwards, in which survivors appear
still bemused by the savagery, have nothing at all to say
for families are inclined to accommodate their casualties –
shoulder-to-shoulder like water they heal over the drowned
so the missing generations have other explanations
than violence: miscarriages; childhood accident; emigration;
or the two dead boys just not in the house the day the shutter fell.
No one knows anything. Not everything need be epic. It is dull, mostly.
At least six rifle or revolver bullets penetrated the bodies
of each of the brothers, who shortly afterwards succumbed to their wounds.
If this were a still familiar Ireland and there was a war on, a war
of a kind that was generous to a moving repertoire of motive and
   profit,
and there were people to kill with no risk to yourself, look for
   Cooneyites.

V

What there is to be won out there among that nation is,
on the one hand, a small worship, a breakfast communion,
every rite alert to children at play below the scarecrow's sacred gibbet
when they bring as one along the lanes to an unknown Heaven
the frugal, anarchic and invaluable gifts of their own selves.
At heart, a mountain discipline on the fertile crescent, of staffs and
   snakes,
meditative on little texts, no bag, no bread, no copper in their money
   belts.
And at the same time is individual and a transgression,
puritan souls transformed in flight with the fidelity of Lir's children,
a disturbance in the air busy with its own magnificence
and visiting upon the complacent clachans the cavalier flourish
of a dispensation as restless as the turning of the earth.

Something is an adventure in there, a quest and a mission
among the spotless, prize-winning farmyards and outhouses.
Two-by-two they went out and preached that people should repent
and the bodies brought by the military to Killermogh
had as mourners only two tall fair women, weeping bitterly.
All this was a long time ago. But it is not fanciful to think of them
  in themselves
as somewhere to lay the head, hole up, hide out, from a world only
  a few fields off,
before the relentless return, by another route, taking nothing at all
  for the road.

Luciano Erba

TRAVELLERS

It's a day of white plumes
of smoke stamped on the sky
from a wind that brings snow
and reddens priests' hands

it's a meadow a bit beyond town
among things in use or disuse
among houses with no balconies
and a railway track's margins

there they dry many bed-sheets
with clothes of different hues
from violet to palest rose

there alongside my train runs
I note down: washing on the lines
plus other womanly signs.

– translated by **Peter Robinson**

Luciano Erba

THE APPLE

The halved apple seems to have
two open eyes in place of its seeds
they smile, look at me, say to me
we're playing, do as you please

if I then quarter my apple
what remains of the seeds is half-closed
it has an angular, angry profile
it's a look without a smile.

– translated by **Peter Robinson**

Aidan Murphy

ACCIDENTAL BLOOD

Last night
I came home
bloodstained.
As I was running
for the last tram
I went down
on my right side,
grazed fingers,
knuckles, hip
and elbow;
nothing serious.

I ran a bath.
I soaked
in liquid heat
for half-an-hour.
How good it felt
after a long night
on the town to be
washing off
blameless,
shameless,
accidental blood.
How wonderful
not to wake
this morning with
a plum-bruised eye
or broken nose.

Aidan Murphy

WRONG SIDE OF TOWN

It was the wrong side of town for pedestrians.

Classic motors took up every inch of kerb-space –
nifty cream models upholstered in suede,
blood-red hotrods with detachable rooftops;
a prideful display of virility in chrome.

It was the wrong side of town for poor dressers.

Unhealthy, in your hand-me-downs, you ambled
in on a traffic of bodies dressed to impress.
Cosmeticised creatures in silver and gold
slipped demurely into taxicabs. Senile codgers,
winking in the windows of The Club Elite,
flashed laser creases, snow-capped teeth.

There was no-one you knew among the retouched faces.
No-one you knew in the lava-lamp-lit doorway of The Bamboo Palace.
No-one you knew muttering prayers and salutations at the parking-
    meters.
No-one you knew drooling the blues into a banged-up Hohner.

It was the wrong side of town for a green, trusting boy.

From your first step over the line you were under the radar,
tracked by the heat of an eye ever-looking
for someone obtrusive like you.
Foolhardy as Christ on the wrong side of the town.

Colette Olney

THAT NIGHT

at four a.m.
they handed me
the overnight-case
that she called her flightbag
and I thanked them
and threw it
on the backseat
and I drove away.
I called on John
and woke him and his girl
and told him that his Gran
was gone; because they said
'she's gone' and something
like a soundless train or plane –
unscheduled, early, which? with her
on board had pulled away
ahead into a fog that wouldn't thicken
or, that wasn't there. Unthinkable
for her to leave without this bag containing
intimate and private things.
So, I drove on...

that overnighter
like a stolen thing – hot,
dangerous, alive behind me
in the car. I tried to enter
into an increasing distance
that I couldn't reach.
I carried on, and carried on –
its dove-soft leather piping,
bright chrome rivets, blue-grey twill,
its handle, like the touch of flesh –
into the dawn. Along the beach,
then down, where the pavilion used to be,
beyond the slip, I cast it out –
and something with it, heavy and unnameable –

and in a breath that came in on a wave
that threw her stepping shape between
the rocks, the shingle and the quay,
her flightbag lightly floated up to me.

Colette Olney

CONDITIONS AT THE TIME
   '...report me and my cause aright / To the unsatisfied', *Hamlet* (Act V, Scene ii)

Outside, the wind was moving through the dead
        weeds by the wall. I took my gun to it. The chimney
spewing smoke. Again I went inside. I told her then
        to leave. To take her sighs away.

At noon, the news was bad. They had my name. I had to
        shut it, butt it, put my double-barrel
to the screen, the windowglass. Jimmy Carty's
        secondhand Scirocco gave a roar, but it was

only in my head – a red gust blasting through.
        The men came crawling then like ants
under the pylons and the trees my father planted
        shuddered and the twin yews creaked.

Not as much as a rook
        or hoodie hurled above the hill. The dull wind
sucked. All day, it raked the field. That night, it shook
        its black self out under the stars. I felt myself

going with it. Yeah, I've heard them say
        a cigarette would have stopped me. Imagine
me saying: 'Don't mind if I do!' –
        biting the tip off and spitting.

I spat all right, a hardcase now –
        my phlegm balled in the wind.
There was no-one to hear me
        and nothing much to change. Not with

that killer on the loose. It's all there
        in the footage: the supposed assassin,
the men hunched, armed; my shadow, thinning
        in the wind. Mam, in her old soft coat – at the edge.

Iggy McGovern

THE CURATE'S EGG

When Sunday Morning Mass is done
The Curate ambles to the door
of Aunt Kay's house: breakfast for one

The Good Room, folding table spread
with linen, china, Apostle spoon
tea cosy and two kinds of bread

The kitchen is a powder keg
of Aunt Kay's efforts to create
the ideal, the *perfect* fried egg

Sausage and bacon mouth dismay
as each flawed sunnyside is chucked
(the village dogs will have their day)

The Father's Love is just and meet
Aunt Kay breaks fast in His Good Room
The Curate labours in the heat.

Josh Ekroy

SNIFFER PATROL

> Under New South Wales law, 'a dog's nose is
> no more than an extension of a police officer.'

Straight to it. I've chased
along scent maps lost to you.
I've traced the warm slick
of your guilt. They're
all banked. I've pawed them.

Reek calls through the dust and spook
of the funnelled crowd
as it heists through the tight street,
can't escape my handled trot.
I'm fledged and led by a relish
that nudges me back and forth.

In the cellars of the dark,
rotten bones tang me,
rouse my curbed chew,
my sprinkle of nose-dew, the thrill
in my belly, sneeze
of muzzle. Stale marrow
is refined, renewed in me.
I truffle the decades.

I can taste all the routes to my truth,
they steal it out of a tic of fur
and convict with a scratch
of my pad. In line-ups
I've yapped a pair of dirty shoes
to solitary.

Mark Roper

OUT OF WATER

Rain nags and needles the pond
but whatever it writes is erased.

At last it loses heart but leaves
a green light over lily-pads

into which a grey wagtail struts,
bent on one thousand prostrations.

Water won't take the repeated
impression of the bird's lemon breast.

No ice is cut by the pond-skater,
no oarprint left by the boatman.

One by one raindrops slide from
a leaf and are never seen again.

Sun lifts his fist and hammers
at the pond's door. No reply.

Water wrinkles its brow, as if
something had slipped its mind.

AN INTERVIEW WITH THOMAS MCCARTHY

Thomas McCarthy in conversation with Catherine Phil MacCarthy

'In those summer days of 1976 and 1977, my head was ablaze with the notion that a poet could make a poem so opaque and iron-clad that a critic who bounced off it would suffer serious injury. I had an architectural obsession with the look of a poem…a poem should be a solid block.' ('Five Summer Afternoons', Gardens of Remembrance*). Where did the notion come from and how did you reconcile it with finding your own poetic voice?*

I think the notion came from reading books like *Another September* by Thomas Kinsella and the revised Dolmen edition of *Poisoned Lands* by John Montague, two poets whose seriousness and sense of vocation I admired enormously. I liked the notion of hardness, of something free-standing like a piece of architecture, because I knew I had a very soft and undisciplined heart. The dominant characteristic of that Dolmen mandarin style was 'high seriousness,' a poetry like a cool Louis le Brocquy.

Poetic voice is a much more problematic thing. I think that's something that can't be altered, unless you want to write like someone else. Yet to write like someone else is a form of cannibalism: why would you want their life as well as your own life? Voice is dirty linen, by washing it out over a lifetime you discover its timbre. Interestingly, the ultimate iron-clad poems came not from Dolmen poets but from the Derek Mahon of *Courtyards in Delft* from Gallery Press. When Seán Dunne and I read that book in the mid 1980s we just gave up trying and went back to our own Waterford lives.

To what extent do you think of art, and poetry in particular as a healing gift? I'm thinking of your poem 'Greatrakes, the Healer' among others.

It is ourselves we nurse. In our poems we find the asylum that heals us. The world is full of bullies. I hate them. I have always hated them. In finding asylum from the bullying of this world, its sickening presumptions in the face of our wanton passivity, we rescue the earth from loneliness, as Derek Mahon intuits. But it is our own earth we rescue. It is that element of the rescued self that the reader observes and follows. The relationship that opens in the text is what calls the sensitive reader indoors. That's where the healing comes in.

When is sincerity/personal expression useless in poetry?

The feelings I record in my first poems are weak because the poetry is poor technically, but they are real feelings. I think the expression of real grief, real love, real rage, is much more successfully carried off in Irish-language poetry. I know I was deeply influenced by Máire Mhac an tSaoi's *Codladh an Ghaiscígh* as well as her earlier love poems like 'Ceathrúintí Mháire Ní Ógáin'. The title poem of the former is one of the greatest lyrics ever written in the twentieth century, comparable with the work of Pasternak or Akhmatova. The surge of love in the poem couldn't be reproduced in the English language. It is the emotional territory of the Gael or a Russian. It is not ironic, it doesn't want to be. I believe sincerity is never useless in such poetry. It means that blood rather than mere ideas flood through the pages in an unembarrassed way. In a bad poem it is wasted, of course, this rush of blood. But it is at the core of our humanity. Sincerity endures with its own kind of power, it is a reminder of our witness. We cannot be sincere for someone else, just as we can't write for someone else.

To what extent do you think there is an anti-lyric movement in contemporary poetry here, similar to what we find in the young Americans, and are you influenced by that?

I'm only influenced by poets I want to read over and over, for their personal music, their emotional intelligence, their fullness. There are really only bad poets and good poets. There's a new generation of astonishingly good poets, I'm thinking of John McAuliffe, Sinéad Morrissey, Alan Moore, Vona Groarke: they've leapt straight into overdrive and renewed Irish poetic practice in a fabulous way. They do a lot of 'thinking in the moment' but there's a mighty circulation of blood inside their poetry. Then there are poets almost of my own generation, Dennis O'Driscoll, James Harpur, Paula Meehan, all producing high voltage stuff. I haven't recognised any anti-lyrical strand, recently. My view is: if it's anti-lyrical, it isn't poetry. It's philosophy. A poem isn't a thing about ideas; there's a heartbeat at the centre of it. There *is* a kind of poetry that's only an arrangement of incidents in thinking, but that's not good enough. What is wonderful is the way poetry renews itself in every generation through these groups of intense new poets. But a challenging, cutting-edge *idea* of poetry is never a poem. I wish people would understand that. The new poets understand that; these new poets have seen how a poem finds its readers without the expensive services of an opinion-broker, an academic commissar. One of the joys of my lifetime has been the moral collapse of literary criticism. Academies and soviets of various kinds used to terrorise poets a generation ago. Now all of that is morally dead. We now live in an era of poetry without passports.

At the end of college, you won a scholarship to Iowa, to the International Writers' Workshop. In what ways were you influenced by that experience?

The Iowa International Writing Programme was a completely life-affirming experience for me. I met nearly forty writers from around the world and spent half a year in rural Iowa with them. It was like an Ark, a survivor of the deluge of the Cold War, and run by an almost John-and-Yoko charismatic couple, Paul Engle and Hualing Nieh. There I met R Parthasarathy and Faiz Ahmed Faiz, Ai Qing and Bien Tse Lin, as well as Americans like Bill Merwin and Marvin Bell. And there I picked up my own copy of Theodore Roethke's *Collected Poems* in the Prairie Lights Bookstore on Dubuque Street. I was so young, only 24. Some of the writers were in their seventies and eighties. I was like a child, and there I met the English poet and Greek scholar, Peter Jay, who has been my publisher for the last 27 years.

What about mask and persona, and isn't there a distance (however slight) between your ordinary speaking voice and your poetic voice?

There is a distance, yes. But that's not my distance. I can't pace it, and a poet doesn't need to. It is the distance between the hours of our lives and the prodigious, parallel accumulation of poems. The poems have a quite distinctive autobiography, selected from our own lives; and I mean *selected*. Your question is a crucial one because it can't be answered. But it can be grasped intuitively, as Seferis grasps it brilliantly when he comments on Stendhal's words about writing day by day and says (in his *Journal*) that daily we live our lives but daily we don't write our poems. Pasternak also, in his *Safe Conduct* warns the reader that 'The poet gives his whole life such a voluntarily steep incline that it is impossible for it to exist in the vertical line of biography...' Biographers should heed that insight in Pasternak.

To what extent is poetry for you a way of redefining reality by your own lights, in opposition to that reality, an escape in the way that you slipped as a child from the meeting rooms to a 'dream- garden'?

I think poetry is a different reality altogether. It is elsewhere. It is not like a newspaper editorial that has strict public duties. It is a world entire to itself with its own centre of gravity, pulling heavy things into it, things like Fianna Fáil in West Waterford and the garden at Glenshelane House where I spent so much time writing my first three books of poetry. Poetry has no duty but it performs – brilliantly and convincingly – a huge public duty by virtue of its having no duty, except to itself. Some poets never get that, do they? You hear all this pub talk and bullshit about the poet's duty. I hate it. I walk away. I'm saturated with politics, but my poems are only interested in that occasionally. Every day I wake up for my poems and for other people's poems, not for politics. The poem, though, by its very selection of subject matter does constantly redefine meanings for me. But I come from an odd working-class family in Cappoquin, a solitary family: I learned as a child to live at a slight angle to the universe, to be quietly and inoffensively odd. I am always in a dream garden; I wake into it and I fall asleep in it. This is my reality, but it doesn't exist in opposition to any other reality. It's just itself, it's just me and the voices that gather around. It's those voices people hear in the poems, but the voices come from people who are both demanding votes and pruning roses.

That reflection continues in The Sorrow Garden *(1981),* The Non-Aligned Storyteller *(1984), and to a lesser extent in later books, and is a meditation on 'Party life', the stifling atmosphere that emanated from meetings. Has your perception of the cumann and the workings of organised politics come at a price, or has it freed you, and to what extent do you feel implicated in a kind of public life and visible world by virtue of being a poet with your work being in the public domain?*

I've always been aware of a ferocious class politics at work in Ireland. It fascinates me: this perpetual dialectic of the Educated *versus* Fianna Fáil. As far as many Fianna Fáil activists are concerned, the constituency is a University and each cumann is a primary degree. An Electoral Area is a Masters, a Comhairle Dáil Ceanntar is a Doctorate. The expelled Deputy is the classic Ambitious Outsider, the Senior Counsel without a Brief. All of these things are mixed up in my memory. I honestly don't try to make sense of it all, at all. But I have paid a heavy price in terms of readers for this Fianna Fáil stuff that surfaces intermittently in my poems. It makes some people really uncomfortable, many readers of poetry in fact. The cumann is a decadent thing, maybe not worthy of poems. But that's exactly what makes me return to it like a moth. Fianna Fáil makes me uncomfortable too, but no inoculation works. I've tried, believe me. It's inside of me like my childhood and it won't go away. It's more than being implicated, it's being inside it all; or underneath it, like a cat under a truck with the engine running. It's the dark side of art, politics, isn't it?

In Gardens of Remembrance *you spoke of 'the necessary phrase' early on, as being 'the fulcrum around which a poem moved'. Is this still the case in* Seven Winters in Paris *(1989), and would you speak about the change in your aesthetic at that stage and how the poems you were writing were changing?*

Between 1984 and 1989 I came closest to not being myself. I was enraged by the failure of Garret FitzGerald's liberal project. I lost faith in the structure of the Dáil and all the Dáil's empty promises of a Republic. I ended up believing in the mirage of an Irish modernism to counteract the meanness of 1980s Ireland. I threw away Kavanagh and Heaney and read Brian Coffey and Denis Devlin. But I soon got over the embarrassment of *Seven Winters in Paris*, I mean the modernist bits. I fear that modernism in Irish writing is just one more Puritan cult, a Jesuitical faction. A poetry that's based only on ideas of poetry is a very thin creature, a lifeless thing. I'm a pro-life poet, rather than a pro-ideas poet; and my life is untidy, foolish, instinctive, maternal, plural. Your poetry is no good if it doesn't allow you to grow old and put on weight, think, your life doesn't need to be refereed by two external examiners. Picasso and Vuillard mean everything to me. They were their own people, untidy like Garret FitzGerald, passionate and possessive like Máire Mhac an tSaoi. That's life for you, not pure, not modern. Just life. Some people never get used to that. It's rather frightening how powerful such people become. The reading of poetry doesn't need to be patrolled. I'm reading Heaney again. He's very much the poet for a mature mind, his measured language, his word-hoard. Kavanagh is now too painful altogether. I think I go to Austin Clarke instead because our native pain is more mediated in Clarke. In Kavanagh it is raw and dreadful; ideas of Ireland when they come to him are like stigmata on the hands of Padre Pio.

The photographer and the camera are rich and complex motifs in your work, and I'm thinking of an early poem 'Form' from The Sorrow Garden, *as well as the title poem, 'The Non-Aligned Storyteller', and the cinema poems in* The Lost Province *that give glimpses of a whole era in Irish life and capture heated comical moments in the local cinema. There is 'No Amarcord to talk about, / no olive trees; no cinematic light.' Yet 'This love we carry is a telephoto lens' ('Here You Are'), and the poems often deliver a world in technicolour, so the uncomforted vision is transformed in poetry?*

I fell in love with a photographer and married her. I was so lucky. But old images haunt me. Maybe it is intensified by working in a library, handling books of images almost every day. Images are such a tight arrangement of incidents, even moving images. When I was an adolescent I fancied myself as a great photographer, I really did. Like old Willy Doyle of

Cappoquin or Rory Wiley of Dungarvan. Then I met a real photographer, Catherine Coakley, who was also a fine writer. That shook me up, I can tell you. She is a genius. The mythical power of images excite me in many ways, but mainly as agents of history, as witnesses of that truth commission. And poetry does throw its light on things. It is a form of illumination, don't forget that.

The novella Merchant Prince *is a fake memoir and a divagation on the influence of poetry on Nathaniel Murphy's life, and a great tribute to four prominent poets who write in the Irish language. Why did you choose this form as a tribute and in what way has working on this novel, and your earlier novels, helped to harness your poetic gift, as well as develop the craft of fiction?*

With me, writing prose clears territory for poetry, like planting a first crop of potatoes to clear the ground. The prose part of *Merchant Prince* was meant to be in footnotes beneath about eighty poems of those great Irish language contemporaries, poets of sublime brilliance, Ó Searcaigh, de Paor, Ó Muirthile and Nuala Ní Dhómhnaill. I'd wanted the texts of the poems to dominate the middle section with footnotes beneath each text in tiny eight-point prose. But those voices would have taken over the book. Instead the middle part is a memory of Nathaniel's reading of these poets, a memoir not of life but of reading. The memory of reading is the real event of that book: the diamonds in Nathaniel's jacket that make him a merchant are really the memories of reading. He is a merchant-poet, a truly attractive kind of Corkman. The shadow at my shoulder for years, a strong ghostly presence and soul companion, was Father Prout, the sophisticated Francis Sylvestor Mahony, Jesuit educated and Ireland's first Joycean, as Joyce knew. Mahony's complex essays are the single greatest achievement of Cork writing in the nineteenth century. Mahony blows all the poetasters of the Young Ireland and Fenian times away with his complexity and his demands upon the educated reader. For me, 'Caoineadh Airt Uí Laoire' and *The Reliques of Father Prout* are the two great Munster texts of the modern era. They are unbeatable. To add just one decent book to that Munster bookshelf is the ambition of my life. It's a struggle and I wonder if I'll ever do it.

There is a vivid account in your memoir of how you sustain writing while work-ing as a librarian: 'I always carry a few used book cards (5cm x 2.5cm) in my top pocket…The genesis of a poem is two or three lines, not necessarily the first lines of the poem. But these lines contain the tone and sense of the poem, as well as some crucial irony or insight. At the end of a working week I used to empty out my pocket, and sellotape the fragments into a notebook. Nothing produces a lyric better than a few fragments, moments of cognition and feeling, rescued from the brain-dead quotidian world of work.' How does the process move from beginning to end and when do you see it as finished?

Where did I write that description? It seems very coherent. Are you sure I wrote that? I must have been in very good form when I wrote that. I think it describes the process very well and doesn't require further explanations. Some things are best left alone. Two or three lines, an insight, something ironic or funny: those are the things that still get me into poetry. Fragments are vital because they're intense little gems. Ideally all poetry should flow from fragments. In my case, if you added the smell of a small petrol engine, a lawn mower or a chainsaw, you'd be certain to get a poem at the end of the day.

You say that 'poetry comes from a kind of magic humanism; a great crush of detail presses in upon the poet's life', and your poems are full of the detail of domestic life, and passionate love. Is that 'magic humanism' a kind of profound pleasure and happiness in being alive, 'a persistent bird of fair weather', or does it mean something else?

Yes, it is a sense of amazement that anything survives, not just myself or my memories. I wonder all the time why we exist, why there is being rather than non-being. Being in this world has a quality of magic to it like the backdrop on a stage or a tight planting of brilliant azaleas. Even now, after thirty years in the library, to switch on all the lights before 9 a.m., to power up all the computers, to log-in to the systems when there's nobody else around; to prepare the space for the day ahead: that has a magical, child-like quality for me. I think I've been doing that all my life, certainly since I was eight years old and living with my blind grandmother. I used to get to the kitchen before her, have the radio on, the fire lighting, the kettle singing. *Voilà*, life. That's how every day begins. I love the first hour of every day. I've never written a poem in the morning, though. With me all the magical humanism belongs to the morning hours, before society enters. Those are the hours without poems, hours of magic humanism. Yes, the early hour is that persistent bird. It sang through my childhood, it sang when my daughter was born. I hope it'll still be singing and hopping about when I'm gone. It'll certainly be in my poems, that persistent fair weather.

Raymond Carver said that apart from the moon and the tides, his children were the greatest influence on his writing life. Would you agree and in what way has being a father influenced the poet?

No. Definitely no, I wouldn't agree. My two children changed my personal life completely, but my writing life was set in stone when I was fifteen or sixteen years old. My view of the poet's life hasn't changed one iota in forty years. I absolutely adore my kids, and admire them both, Kate Inez and Neil. But I believe strongly that we shouldn't lean on our children, they owe us nothing. They are at the beginning of their own long adventures in life. Leave them alone, I say. I've written about them, so they do exist in the world of my poems, but I wouldn't expect them to be an influence on my writing life. They are very calm persons, and they think of me as a very odd, unconventional individual, not because I'm a poet but because I'm from Cappoquin. They are urban creatures, Cork people. As a father, of course, you have massive hopes for them and immense fatherly expectations.

> The voyage to Italy and other places is central in Merchant Prince, and travel is an important motif in the new poems in Mr Dineen's Careful Parade. This is in contrast to the theme of emigration in earlier poems, where travel is associated with dispossession and loss. To what extent are you reclaiming a dimension of Irish culture often forgotten, in Merchant Prince, that began in ancient times and to what extent do you take inspiration more from rootedness than travel?

I'm a very rooted creature. If I could get away with it, I'd never leave my small vegetable patch in Cork. When I was a child I never wanted to leave my grandmother's kitchen in Barrack Street, Cappoquin. When I was a young man I never wanted to leave Brigadier FitzGerald's house and garden at Glenshelane. It is worse than being rooted: I'd say it's a medical condition. The town of my early childhood was emptied of people by emigration; I first travelled from Cappoquin to reconnect with my English cousins and my sister who'd gone to do nursing in England. Now I seem to travel where others are from. I was in Hungary recently. It was like being back in Ireland in 1962, except I was having lunch in a nuclear power station between Reactor Two and Reactor Four! For us in Ireland travel has changed from being a net loss to a net gain. What is poignant for all Irish people is to see our story replayed now in the lives and travels of our new immigrant communities. In them we meet ourselves again. We say hello to our fathers and mothers. Who could have imagined that that would ever happen? What would the late John Healy say, or Peadar O'Donnell or even old Bishop Lucey? We have been blessed in our own lifetimes. Blood from outside is good, as Máire Mhac an tSaoi observed in her poem 'Codladh an Ghaiscígh.' Immigration makes us strong. Remember, we are witnessing the first massive inward migration of a people into Ireland who don't want to kill us or take our land. That must mean something special. It's a sure sign that we're not dying. I just wish that someone like John Healy had lived to see it all: I keep imagining the columns he might have written. I haven't a clue about what's reclaimed in *Merchant Price*: I was just bringing home a merchant-poet, Nathaniel Murphy, from the long-ago to the present-day reader. We've been blessed in so many ways. We live in a rich land and an important part of that Irish richness is the memory of elsewhere. To misquote Flaubert, we carry this genetic code of our exile like a cemetery within.

Anzhelina Polonskaya

BULLFINCHES

If you close the door – bullfinches pop out
of the silence within all the tile roofs.

And here I hung a cage of such languor
that my bullfinches are leaving one by one.

Your father's house will be like a rag in a fire,
your cruel son's grown up and you're doubly alone.

How can you stay sane in this war or that?
You must know that your love is your prison.

I'll return from the walls and enter the more terrifying walls,
here you won't consider my craft a labour.

So I'll end up like you found me:
a stone, blind and deaf – nearby or far away.

– translated by **Andrew Wachtel**

Máighréad Medbh

PARTING SONG
  – in memory of Bridgie Kelly, Achill Island

Out here we all sing,
ravens, crows or linnets, wooden flutes or foghorns.
Shed skin, chestnut-smooth or orange-peel-puckered,
tight as a drum or saggy as an elephant,
all sends its tune, little ingénue, small starter
among the skies.

Listen to you now
on your deathbed, frail woman with the sweet voice.
'Prop me up, I want to sing my song.'
And you do. You're hardly more than eyes,
two shiny chestnuts in a leafless tree,
but your voice is as clear as the air out here.

Out here we all sing.
You know we do. We've been your backing.
When you sang 'Eileen MacMahon'
among the pans, dusted with flour,
the tide you felt was the rush of our voices
buoying you, your own personal sea.

Bridgie Kelly,
married young and widowed early,
always half-widowed, your husband a migrant worker;
you were sometimes in your voice,
sometimes in your tears,
sometimes in your hands, a brief rainbow.

Out here we all sing,
enemies and bosom pals. Faceless, we're not concerned
with placing or privilege.
You'll be side by side with Maria Callas, small diva,
big as a goddess despite your short path
from cottage to hill and back.

You could say we don't care
and that we care the best. All words with no tone.
But when the flesh starts to flag as it does now,
we're thrilled as midwives at every birth.
Here's the head, oh yes it's coming, and the first cry
is a melody, little novice, brave starter
upon our wings.

Anthony Caleshu

IN CASE OF FLOOD

'Some men die at ebb tide; some at low water; some at the full of the flood;
– and I feel now like a billow that's all one crested comb... I am old; – shake
hands with me, man.' – Herman Melville, *Moby Dick*

Never once have I witnessed such a display of camaraderie, but I
have read about them a lot: mostly in *The Oxford Book of the Sea*. In
The Oxford Book of the Sea, you can read stories which will engross
you. The passage I just read to you is not from the *Oxford Book*, but
I think you'll agree that it is engrossing nonetheless. There is nothing
so elemental as water. Water has no past prejudices. In the case of
too much water I have mapped out the quickest escape route from
the five most common places to stand in this office. I don't think
you'll be surprised to hear that one of the escape routes requires
that you don't move at all. You just keep sitting at your desk, and
wait patiently for the taste of salt which you've been craving all
your life.

– from the sequence 'What Makes Thee Want To Go A Whaling, Eh?'

Ian Pople

AUTHENTICATIONS

Against a blue sky, a weather
vane and red-tiled roof;
the smell of pruned cypress
makes it feel more homely

and cast in the smell
of wet summer, the smell
of feed mill pulled deep
into the lungs of a girl

running for the bus
and a man crossing the lines
where the track curves
beyond beech trees.

Oliver Dunne

ICARUS

'Why did Icarus fall?'

'His pride, father.'

'And what else?'

'His love of young men.'

'And what else?'

'His bragging, father.'

'And what else?'

'He wrote beautiful poems.'

Jean O'Brien

UNCHARTED LANES

We could travel all the redbrick lanes
behind houses in roads with name like
Palmerston, Windsor or Ormond;
they had no ordinance, did not appear on maps
or not the ones we were using, we could spy into the backs
of houses that from the front gave nothing away.
Here were old shed doors painted cherry red or apple green
or galvanised steel garage doors that went 'up and over'.
From where we walked we could see into scullery windows
and gardens that had apple trees, or bushes of gooseberries
or trees with swings hung from them.
Some gardens sported a snagged tennis net.

Sometimes we'd see a pond overgrown with mossy
stones half submerged and we could spy
into a garden shed, its cobwebbed junk taking
on a significance not found in our own sheds.
That cardboard box with faded writing
must contain something more precious than old/
new kitchen tiles that were surplus to requirements.
We liked the uncharted lanes and byways, only children
and dogs in a hurry used them. Once a terrible man,
dressed in a greatcoat and wheeling a bicycle came along,
he had one hand on the saddle and the other tugged
at his swollen member. This made us remember
to hurry home for tea. We never spoke about it later
and never told our mothers, we would not have had
the words.

Louise C Callaghan

DYNAMO

Why is it that every dream seems *strange?*
And when you write it out it starts to slip,
like quicksilver, the drops of mercury
our father'd bring home in a small glass tube
from his auto-parts factory workshop.
The mercury'd escape in the blankets
and be lost somewhere in your lap –
or drop into the furrow of the carpet.
You let it out, that was that. Excitement
always turned to loss. And then on your page
there would be nothing to read, only this:
you know last night I had the strangest dream!

Cian Macken

SNOW

Down at the docks
The moon was out and
A ship was leaving
For Brazil, at three o'clock
And we held colds hands
As a foghorn called
And mast lights
Sparked together
As our phones
Filled up with questions,

We found
Three white steps
To sit on and
You stretched
Your knees out straight
And when we kissed
It seemed
Quiet enough for snow.

Gerard Smyth

REMNANT

The ark that sheltered us submits to ruin,
neglect, abandonment. There's a ghostly ambience
where chattels have vanished, where mornings
of motherhood had their own chronology.

It happens by stealth: the ark that sheltered us
becomes a remnant of the past, unroofed, stripped bare
as if a thief passed through it taking everything
but the black shadows, the creak on the stair.

Doors are padlocked to their frames
– doors to which contagion came
to give the loudest knock: scarlet fever, whooping cough.

That familiar room where time has stopped,
was birth-place, sickbay, nursery – a zone of memory
behind frosted glass. Light from street-lamps

shone in at night illuminating folded garments,
household objects: the butter, golden in its dish,
the stove-lid blackened with a rub of polish.

Gerard Smyth

IN THE BRAZEN HEAD

Under the image of the rebel on the scaffold,
perhaps on the very spot where the plot was hatched,
we sat in a corner of the Brazen Head,
spent long evenings until we came to the dregs,
sharing the company of men of all trades,
fellow-travellers in from the cold, in from the rain,
from nights of frost and the four winds passing
through places soon to be rubble, sites of desecration.
We sat in a Cupid's corner, eavesdropping
on raw music in the backroom: banjo and whistle,
and the balladeers swilling songs
from the cup of tradition: 'Boulevogue', 'The Foggy Dew'.
All the listeners keeping time, tapping the tunes.

Patrick Maddock

BOXES

It's too late now to let her face muscles fall slack:
it's half-past-five and the sun has already set.
She knows this isn't the shortest day she's met
– she can thank the god of the seasons for that.
Her heart still beats as the key sits in the lock
to the inside room where his movables are stacked
– cardboard metropolis, consortium of boxes,
his name in clear marker, sticking-tape at the flaps.
One day he'll have to take them away and go back
where he's gone. For her, it can't come soon enough.
When he calls, she'll stand off – watch him in and out,
as he leaves her more space (if it's space she lacks)
where she may feel at liberty, relieved of this pulp,
to smile at the walls until she's brightened them up.

Marie Coveney

SCISSORS

I emerged from the birth canal
of a dark mill.
In a kitchen drawer
of blunt instruments I lay open,
blooded by the first probing finger.
I snip, I sever, I slit, I score
I am invincible, precision steel
to the core.
The things that I undo
cannot be undone.
I have sisters
who pink for a living,
all crocodile jawed and heavy metal
they crunch at the skirts
of women.
I lust after long-haired girls
tossing rope-manes
down their backs.
I want to unburden them
to expose what I desire most,
the nape
in all its simplicity.

I have French-dreams
of bloodied wicker-baskets.

Noël Hanlon

MILLING ABOUT

The old rooster, having proclaimed
too many times, long before and after
dawn – *the sun has risen*, switches
to his other job on earth, to tell
the hens when he's found remnants
of green in the scratched-brown coop-yard.
And they, with their useless wings lifted,
race to him with their hunger, answering,
I'm coming! I'm hungry! The young rooster,
holds back, he knows to test his tiny, red-crowned-glory
in the shadows of the coop, his tenuous crowing
where the old rooster is not. And the Aracanas,
wilder, like grounded hawks, are silent,
do not mingle with the hybrids
– the Red Sex Links or the black and white
Lacewings – they choose the quiet instead,
find the furthest corners of the coop to hide
their jewels, their delicate blue-green eggs,
while the brown and white layers squabble
over who shall get the best (warmest?) boxes
to lay in. Indignant ruckuses erupt, someone
has pushed someone out of a broody nest,
someone is being hen-pecked, insulted or assaulted.
All the while, the kind old rooster continues
searching for scraps, muttering promises,
with such undying hopefulness and devoted focus
that the hens continue to mill around him.
And then it will happen, with some unseen tilt
of hours in his eye, he cries out, *Daylight's going!*
One by one then they straggle back into the coop,
long before night, as if sunlight makes sound
safe. While it drops, they gather into a silence.
Except for the thump of talons clamping on
roost-beams, or the whoosh of settling
domesticated wings, there is only the murmuring –
as close as chickens ever come to singing –
of peace.

Noël Hanlon

CLIMBING ABOVE HELL ROARING CREEK

Ascending the red pumice mountain,
as if drawn to the most difficult
to reach, we leave the effortless meadows
of mariposa lilies and quenching springs,
go further, where there are no trails,
but faded flags, only I seem to see,
waving from the sparse arms of trees.
You call me when you lose sight of me.

The mountain turns my name
around in its hard mouth and swallows.
You follow me through the opening into
the red bowl of a sleeping volcano.
We share the precious last drops of water,
where no one could stay longer than moments,
though the view from here tells us everything
about beginnings and exposed betweens.

Our breathing twines in the final effort,
carries us back to the oval body
of water where I strip and swim across
while you carry my clothes and walk around
the lip of the lake edged with reeds that bend
from the weight of blue, mating dragonflies.
We meet on the other side where we have tied
our single kayak, where we share a fire.

Geraldine Mitchell

THE INVISIBLE GIRL

You saw me as curtain, carpet,
the floral pattern of my dress
disappearing into background
like a lizard on a rock.

You thought I was 'just a child'
living in my childish head.
You took my silence for an absence.
Mistook me for my doll.

But my eyes saw, my ears heard,
my nose picked up
the layered scent of adult talk.
You paid no heed to the girl,

what pictures she was painting
on the inside of her skull,
how she smelt the rotting flowers,
could taste the brine of adult tears.

Joseph Allen

THE ADULTERER

I remember that unexpected bus trip,
my mother silent
and, unusual for a week day,
dressed in her finery.

Marching through the village,
being dragged along by the hand
impatient at my slowness,
even then I knew
it wasn't really me she was angry with.

She rapped on the door,
sounds amplified in the crisp morning air,
I noticed the fear
on the features of the women who opened.

An uncle in his vest, bare feet,
heard with shock
the death of his wife.

On the bus home
I sensed she was crying,
her arm pulling me
close to her.

Terry McDonagh

BY THE *ALSTER PAVILLON* IN HAMBURG

Late morning in a good life. I have my back
to the *Pavillon* & my face to
the flat autumn water of the Alster.

Swans out there nudge the verges & gardens
of Schwanenwik. Inside, there's Ostfriesen tea,
cordials & exotic coffees for regular &

passing trade. Boats sway in their shackles.
I'm exiled in a picture on a sunny Saturday
in November with an Irish Harp in my head.

I turn to the city to face Hamburg; to
a flock of seagulls among spires
dipping & diving into the Rathausmarkt.

They could have been from anywhere.
There's a horse-cart in a shed behind
a house in Ireland. Heavy loads are done.

An old man stands by the shed wall, talking
to himself, passing on old ways to the wind.
He's waiting to be called in for tea.

I imagine I had a wild child's head, ready wings
& feet to land anywhere. I'll be going to
the football later. A breeze with a sharp edge

will blow up the pitch. Is that the same wind
that blew the roof off our granary? There were
steps up but the floorboards were rotten.

If I had gone through the floor,
I'd have ended up among cows.
Now is a good time to stop.

Benjamin Keatinge

JUST FOLLOWING THE CURVE OF THE WORLD

Harry Clifton, *Secular Eden* (Wake Forest University Press, 2007), $15.95.

Justin Quinn begins his recent book on *Modern Irish Poetry 1800-2000* with the question 'What is "Irish poetry"?', and he goes on to suggest that contemporary Irish poets have abandoned 'the nation as a framework for Irish poetry'. Quinn argues that many contemporary poets are fundamentally 'uninterested in the historical fate and crises of Ireland in the twentieth century'.

Born in 1952, Harry Clifton's ancestry includes nationalist insularity on his father's side as well as South American internationalism on his mother's side and his poetry could be said to reflect these conflicting roots. Rather than choosing to engage with his homeland on its own terms, Clifton has chosen to travel and his poems draw from extended stays in Africa, Asia and various European countries, most recently, France. When asked in an interview with David Wheatley about his travels and his relationship to Ireland, Clifton responded by saying that: 'the more I have travelled, the more I have come to see the poet's true home as language rather than place. I would describe myself more as a citizen of language rather than a citizen of place.'

Clifton's most recent volume *Secular Eden* is the fruit of his refusal to answer Quinn's question 'What is "Irish poetry"?' *Secular Eden* simply sidesteps the issue and is an exemplary case of the new internationalism in Irish poetry. But Clifton has been writing in this vein for many years now from his early collections *Office of the Salt Merchant* (1979) and *Comparative Lives* (1982) up to his more recent selected poems *The Desert Route* (1992) as well as *Night Train Through the Brenner* (1994), all published by Gallery. But this latest volume *Secular Eden* (2007) has brought Clifton's singular poetic gifts to wider public attention and Clifton received the *Irish Times* Poetry Now festival award in April 2008 for this collection. If recognition of Clifton has been slow, one suspects that he has been fortified by his comparative invisibility, especially given his poetic interest in the gaps between public reward and private poetic integrity. As Clifton writes of the Romanian poet Benjamin Fondane, a victim of the Holocaust:

> And now they tell me 'Hide your poems, wait –
>   Somewhere in Nineteen Eighty
> Readers will find you...' I see a Paris street,

Old letterbox, a drop-zone for the infinite
In a leaf-littered hallway, where a publisher long ago
Went out of business, and a young man searches
In the sibylline mess and the overflow
For a few lost words...
        – 'BENJAMIN FONDANE DEPARTS FOR THE EAST'

This magisterial meditation on history and the Holocaust is on a par with Derek Mahon's 'A Disused Shed in County Wexford' in its evocation of the lost and broken generations who have been defeated by history. Clifton's historical intelligence could be compared with Polish masters of the genre, Zbigniew Herbert or Czesław Miłosz in the historical weight of his poetry. We find echoes of poems like Herbert's 'Report from the Besieged City' in the grandeur and urgency of Clifton's historical themes.

If Clifton's poetic canvass is mainly situated west of Warsaw, with Paris as its fulcrum, there is nonetheless a good deal of Mitteleuropa in these poems. Clifton creates 'ciphers of exile' ('White Russians') which, in poem after poem, speak of the condition of not-belonging and of transit and travel. For Clifton, we are all 'passengers, time-travellers' who 'Waft through another twentieth century' ('Lódz'). The nightmare of history is cross-referenced in Clifton's magnificent closing poem 'Benjamin Fondane Departs for the East', but the signature of the volume as a whole is 'That well-known little-spoken-of discreet / Establishment on the Street of the Four Winds' ('The Street of the Four Winds') where fugitive private and public lives converge. These poems range from north to south, east and west, from Europe to Ireland to Asia and Australia. There are no limits to Clifton's cultural curiosity and the 'old, shipwrecked life' ('Staggering Ashore') of both homeland and exile is repeatedly re-examined and worked through. Indeed, for Clifton, exile is a necessary condition of our humanity and so the dialectic of home versus abroad is no longer relevant. Exilic sentiment looms large in poems about Ireland and any kind of home is always provisional and fugitive, a prelude to a new beginning elsewhere.

However, Clifton made a home for himself in Paris through much of the 1990s when these poems were written and Paris is very much the anchor city of the volume. And so, in 'To the Fourteenth District', Clifton pays homage to a particular *arrondissement* where the poet lived and which other exiles have also made their home, among them: Beckett, Giacometti, Lenin, Salvador Dali. It is an in-between place housing people in transit, a temporary abode perhaps, but also a home of sorts:

...A mile to the east
The Chinese quarter, west the electrified trains

Of Montparnasse. But in between,
A little left of centre, the *quatorzieme*,
All softness of acacia trees, and plane-trees,
Living off its pavements.

– 'TO THE FOURTEENTH DISTRICT'

All the iconography of Paris is here:

. . . the restaurants,
Ethnic, local, and the pubs,
The Russian bookstore, with its *émigré* texts,
The pretty, unapproachable women
Of the Latin Quarter, Sunday morning heat,
The *philosophes*, bohemian, effete,
The whole back catalogue of modern jazz...

– 'MONT SAINTE-GENEVIEVE'

Paris as cosmopolitan centre and gathering place of *émigré* cultures (Anglophone, Russian), especially during the inter-war period (but equally now), is of key interest for Clifton. Paris is an everywhere and a nowhere, a cosmopolitan heartland but also disorientating in its very diversity. It is therefore representative of the cultural mix of any modern city, except that Paris has a much longer tradition of diversity and intellectual freedom than Dublin or even London.

There is an uncanny emptiness in this twenty-first century urban space with 'The millions of strange people / Whirled like atoms through the hub of Montparnasse' ('Reductio') as well as 'the lit conceptual cages' ('Reductio') of meeting places – 'Dome, Select, Rotonde' – and private dwellings. Paris is the city of the *flâneur*, the city of impermanent private lives, social fragmentation or the great, good international city, depending on your point of view. Some of these poems exhibit the same cosmopolitan *tristesse* as Auden's 'September 1, 1939' where the 'Faces along the bar / Cling to their average day' amidst the 'Negation and despair' of history. But there are also many attempts to make connections across the cosmopolitan space so that:

The traffic, birds, pneumatic drills
Of an absolute city
Will be yours...

[...]

To do with as you please.
Ideal objects, the people, the trees,
Giving themselves unconsciously...
– 'WHEN THE PROMISED DAY ARRIVES'

Here is home. It is a compromised place where an awareness of cultural relativity is important. Clifton is 'not the first' to be here and he 'will not be the last' and his 'Disillusionments, lost years / Are part of the story', as he puts it in 'When the Promised Day Arrives'. But throughout *Secular Eden*, Paris as a physical space, but also as a cultural emblem, takes on the historical baggage of exile and belonging which Clifton repeatedly explores.

Another feature of the great, good international city is its secularism. We live in a post-religious age and Clifton examines the consequences of our loss of faith. God is now characterised by his 'absences, abscondings, abdications' ('God in France') and Clifton explores what has come to replace him. The secular life is limited, it is bounded by mundane horizons, but it is also edenic in its realism and practicality. So even a simple poem 'Lighting Up', which describes a woman drinking coffee and smoking in a Paris café, takes on an epiphanic depth:

It is one of those days
Of wintry light, transfiguring everything
Like a nimbus.

[...]

A page turns, in the history of being,
Unconscious, but aware.
– 'LIGHTING UP'

Of course, Clifton is aware of the magnitude of what has been lost as well as gained and he has taken religion as a point of departure in earlier poems such as 'Death of Thomas Merton' (in *Comparative Lives*, 1982) and 'The Typhoid Priest' (in *The Liberal Cage*, 1988). If these earlier poems feature beleaguered literary Catholics facing up to an intolerable world, *Secular Eden* explores a world where faith has ceased to matter and the lived, earthly life, with its pleasures and disappointments, takes on a new significance. Paris is the capital city of the new secularism where God is 'Adrift on the everyday' ('God in France'). Clifton re-imagines God as a latter-day *flâneur*, mingling with a crowd and enjoying the discreet anonymity of the twenty-first century city.

If Clifton reserves a vatic authority for some of his more substantial poems about history, he also has a keen eye for the everyday. We are, he suggests, 'all of us transmigrating / Like souls, through the neutral space on the map' ('Benjamin Fondane Departs for the East'). The 'neutral space' turns out to be the Promised Land of Biblical prophecy transmuted into the secular space of the modern city. When Benjamin Fondane arrives in the East, he finds 'the real Apocalypse' which is foreshadowed and contrasted by:

> ...*Pitchipoi*
> As the wits describe it, after the Yiddish tale –
> A village in a clearing, zlotys changed for francs,
> Children at their books, the old and frail
> Looked after...
> — 'BENJAMIN FONDANE DEPARTS FOR THE EAST'

So Clifton offers us a counterpoint of historical nightmare in which the 'people of the Book' are exterminated set against the current secular Eden of French society in the late twentieth century where, at the very least, children are educated and the old and frail are looked after. The 'other world we are asked to believe in' ('Benjamin Fondane Departs for the East') is not just an ironic Yiddish tale but also a substantial reality in the civilised environment of modern day Paris.

So, our contemporary secular Eden is represented as a blank space where:

> No-one will ever fall from grace
> Where the bells are electric, and the chimes
> Of a French municipal hall
> Preserve us in time.
> — 'SECULAR EDEN'

But this harmonious blank space is underwritten and shadowed by the blank space of unimaginable historical atrocity, the Holocaust, which circumscribes and conditions any feelings of present day contentment in our modern environment. We can rejoice now in the everyday:

> A rattle of skateboards –
> Children playing. There go lovers,
> Crossing race and bloodline. And the flight-paths
> Write their celestial Word
> On the sky above us...
> — 'SECULAR EDEN'

But the celestial Word of past times has often been an agent of intolerance with the Holocaust as the most grievous example, amongst many, of religious and ethnic hatred. The fact that bloodlines no longer matter, at least in contemporary Paris, is a merciful development and a welcome feature of the Promised Land. Through his attention to history, Clifton shows what we can be grateful for. By reminding us of the unbearable horror of twentieth-century history, Clifton also endorses the unbearable lightness of the contemporary city.

Thomas McCarthy

MEMOIR AND CELEBRATION

David Marcus, *Lost and Found: Collected Poems* (New Island Books, 2007),
€14.95.
John Jordan, *Selected Poems* (Dedalus Press, 2008), €14.

These two books under review, with their attendant sense of memoir
and celebration, are intimately bound up with the history and heritage of
Poetry Ireland. That very phrase, or composite expression, 'Poetry
Ireland' belongs to the mind of the venerable David Marcus. It was his
poetic, passionate and blessedly naive young self who first published
Poetry Ireland in 1948, continuing as an offshoot of *Irish Writing*. Marcus
was born into a still-active Cork business circle of picture dealers and
framers; and the compelling impulse of his life has been to frame, to
preserve, to anthologise or edit the passing literary moment. But, as the
Waterford writer George O'Brien points out in his very sensitive and
lucid Introduction, 'In addition to his many other literary accomplishments,
David Marcus is also a poet, and indeed as a young man devoted a good
deal of his literary energy to verse, and...was at that time "convinced," as
he ruefully records in *Oughtabiography*, "I was the best unpublished poet
in Ireland under twenty-one."'
    The energy of the young poet, the musical and compelling refrains of
the Cork poetic Fifties, is seen in poetry like 'Punchinello' :

> But crown was lost, and throne was lost,
> > And sceptre, sway, and court were lost
> And queen was lost – and there I was,
> > An ordinary thing.

[...]

> But sometimes when the night is cold
> > And half the moon is pale and old,
> I build myself a fire of gold,
> > And sit like this and stare.

Such a poetic does place Marcus unquestionably among the neo-Romantics
of divine music like Dylan Thomas or among poets of a Lorca-like incan-
tation like Patrick Galvin. Other poems reprinted here, 'The Ten Roads
to My Love,' 'Barriers' or 'Love's House,' speak of those post-War out-

of-time essences, the phenomenal consolations of ecstatic love that creates 'A holiday in the heart, / And a Sabbath in the soul.' Love is the one thing unambiguously associated with poetry: it is Marcus's guiding impulse, as O'Brien points out: 'the passion and hunger for attachment.' Even the works of translation here, poems from the Irish tradition, contain recurring phraseology of love lost or love unattainable: 'Three things through love I see' or 'My grief that I'm not / with the one I love best' or 'Then I catch sight of my love' – all of these poems are passionate with a hunger for attachment. This motif is so compelling, and possibly a major impulse behind his translation of 'The Midnight Court'. It is also an impulse that widens out into a series of social matrices in his two best prose works, *To Next Year in Jerusalem* and *A Land Not Theirs*. Just as Marcus seems compelled to frame and anthologise general literary achievements of his Irish milieu, from Trumpet Books to the *Irish Press*, he has framed as a poet the bustle of love from the 1940s to the present. This 'Collected' is also a very successful act of framing: it places a golden border around a life well-spent in literature. While most of his Jewish contemporaries, and nearly all of the highly-educated Jews of Cork, left Ireland after the War, many to set up a new home in a new Israel, Marcus came back to Ireland to plough a lonelier furrow and pick many of the impoverished lilies in the field from our literary Mucker. *Lost and Found* is an important book, now; actually, it's one of those canny, crucial books that somehow complete our posterity. It will sit there to remind coming generations that part of the literary gallery of post-Emergency Ireland is occupied by a poet from the tribe of Mr Bloom, a poet with a unique story to tell, and many of these unique stories were told in unique poems:

> My people come from a far-off land
> And bear the mark of the burning-brand.
>
> But words are useless. They do not speak.
> My people turned the other cheek.
>
> Who are my people? I search my mind
> And remember Donne who was all mankind.
>
> – 'FRATRICIDE'

While it may be said that David Marcus never crossed over to the land of the Jordan, a Jordan did cross over to David Marcus. That Jordan was none other than John Jordan: which brings us to the second book under review, John Jordan's *Selected Poems*. Writing here in his superb Introduction, the poet Hugh McFadden reminds us 'that had John Jordan not created the magazine *Poetry Ireland* out of the ashes of the Fifties journal *Irish Writing*...then the world of literary magazines in Dublin might not have developed as it did from the Sixties to the present time: in particular, Poetry Ireland itself as a society, and the *Poetry Ireland Review*, might not have come into being at all...' What the scholarly and scrupulous Jordan had perceived, as McFadden hints, is that the evidence of real, continuing work, day-to-day work of an ordinary literary kind, is the surest bulwark against Irish conservatism and reactionary, dispiriting Dublin bitterness of the old variety.

Jordan was certainly a brilliant man. Listening to him expound upon the varying merits of Flann O'Brien, Anthony Cronin or John Montague in the Long Valley Bar in Cork many years ago, I remember being startled and overwhelmed by his trenchant memory, his insistent mischief and the diamond-edge nature of even his most casual opinions. It must have been good to be alive when these guys were undergraduates. He was as colourful as Micheál MacLiammóir, but formally educated, with the robust insights of a good scholar ('Would you ever check in those library records of yours and see if there were ever Wilmores resident at Cork,' were his parting words to me at Glanmire Station. Except that he didn't part. He must have got off the train because he was back in the Long Valley snug when I returned that evening). He was searching, there, I guess, for the one good bowl of soup:

> Among the blazing azaleas
> Of the Parque del Campo Grande
> I perceived the true, sophisticated
> Marxist point of view:
> Let the people have duck soup...
> — 'FOR JULIUS HENRY MARX (1891-1977)'

So well-educated was he, indeed, that unhappiness and pain had to be expressed in a complex way, in the manner of Austin Clarke:

> All the rest of it is maculate:
> Clerical quip and liberal mind,
> Perspectives of eternity which we're told
> Art can find...
> — 'HOMAGE TO THE PSEUDO-JANSENIUS'

He was part of that generation most enriched and most damaged by the conditions of Irishness. Never before had a generation of intellectuals come to maturity when the Irish Catholic world-view held such sway. There was a complete orthodoxy and social tidiness, an insanity of completion that bordered on spiritual tyranny. Yeats was too recent then; the detritus of his last arguments were still hanging around the foyers, and Joyce, even the Joyce of the *Portrait*, was hardly absorbed. Help was on the way. America would open as a possibility, but too late for Jordan as for Clarke. Jordan's poetry, therefore, is a splintered and damaged literature, with huge lumps of flesh knocked out of his possible genres and aesthetic from battles with that overwhelming orthodoxy, Catholic Dublin. Like others, his poetry would have to live on lack, as Austin Clarke put it – 'I have my nuances and Chekovian glooms', Jordan wrote in 'Second Letter: To Patrick Swift', and such glooms were personal, sexual and political. There is more than Dublin wit; there is something profoundly sad in:

> *Dixit:* I don't like the use of that word 'bottom'.
> *Dixit:* It's about time we
> Learnt that the heart's no pincushion.
>
> And then, you know, he put out the light,
> And they went to bed and were unhappy ever after.
> — 'A SEDUCTION OF THE '40S'

But there you have it: that struggle to have a personal life, a personal imagination. In Jordan you have a poet conscious of the general malaise that pervaded Ireland and post-War Europe, as Hugh McFadden wrote, as well as a civilised man's considered statement to the moment, as Macdara Woods has observed. John Jordan was all of these things and more. He had limitless potential, like Dublin itself, and a good deal of what he wished to say is in these beautiful pages from Dedalus Press. His voice was so clear and beautiful, a cornet solo above the noise of mere opinions. When he spoke it was always so meaningful and oracular. It is impossible to believe that he has been gone these twenty years.

Peter Pegnall

ALSO CHUCKLES AND JOY

Daljit Nagra, *Look, We Have Coming to Dover!* (Faber and Faber, 2007), £8.99.

If you are given a label, tear it off, shred it. Poets may not be unacknowledged legislators, but they are inveterate outsiders. You might not divine that at a literary soirée, where all too often the natter is crammed with facile ambition rather than dangerous, enduring ideas; but look at a poet's work and you will be able to sense and judge the rich, the individual, 'the real thing'.

Daljit Nagra is a poet who knows the publicist's efforts to package, the phrase-maker's compulsion to pigeonhole, the educator's itch to explain, to incorporate. He will be no tribal representative, at the same time as addressing the snares and possibilities of family, social and cultural life. He bears witness, he does not pontificate. Consider his sardonic awareness of fame at a price:

> Should I foot it featly as a Punjab in Punglish
> Sold on an island wrecked by the British
>
> Did *you* make me for the gap in the market
> Did *I* make me for the gap in the market
>
> Does it feel good in the gap in the market
> Does it feel gooey in the gap in the market...
> — 'BOOKING KHAN SINGH KUMAR'

The way he combines cod Elizabethan with stand-up rhetoric, the way he tumbles into the bathetic: this is genuine wit, fully digested anger:

> Should I talk with the chalk of my white inside
> On the board of my minstrel – blacked outside
>
> Should I bleach my bile-name or mash it to a stink
> Should I read for you straight or Gunga Din this gig...

The lack of punctuation is telling, although the poem ends with an exclamation mark, that most adolescent of devices:

More than your shell-like, your clack applause

What bothers is whether you'll boo me if I balls

Out of Indian!'

Daljit Nagra teaches English at a London Secondary School, so is compelled to promulgate the condescensions of the G.C.S.E. 'Anthology', in which 'multi-culturalism' is a badge, a liberal mantra which replaces quality with relevance, art with slogan. His regulated, mischievous venom finds a fiery, mimicked voice in 'Kabba Questions the Ontology of Representation, the Catch 22 for "Black Writers"...':

> Vy giv my boy
> dis freebie of a silky blue
> GCSE antology with its three poets
> from three parts of Briten – yor HBC

> Of Eaney, Blake,
> Clarke, showing us how
> to tink and feel? For Part 2, us
> as a bunch of Gunga Dins ju group, *'Poems*

> *from Udder Cultures*
> *and Traditions'.* 'Udder' is all
> vee are to yoo, to dis cuntry...

Nagra is perfectly aware of what it is to be part of a heterogeneous, shifting experience, but time and again he resists the notion that identity can be fixed, can subsume the wilder reaches of imagination, the glories of technique:

> Yoo teachers are like
> dis Dalgit-Bulram mickeying
> of me as Kabba. I say for di garment
> of my voice may be sestina, sonnet, tanka,

> tum-ti-tum
> wid best vurds please!

Coleridge would have approved.

This is not primarily a political collection, however. There is a range and depth of feeling which is itself enough to ditch easy definitions or polemic. Friendship shivers through 'Sajid Naqvi', an elegy for a student colleague, who died of a 'freak heart attack'. Nagra recalls a young man who'd

> ...sit nocturnally
> crunching his way through Maths equations with The Smiths.

At the funeral, such moments are side-lined, as

> ...someone croaked endless hymns from the Koran.

And his divorced mother is forbidden to show up. Nagra screams in silence against the appropriation of a complex person by a bleak ritual; but somehow he achieves a tenderness and almost-contact in a final possessive pronoun, in a name:

> ...We shadowed the hearse outward through narrow
> roads, winding up in deepest Surrey, at a Shi'ite cemetery

> where the prayers raged again, chanting over his lowered
> coffin, hitting the box with force of the hard soil
> his family threw, as they tucked away our Saj.

Unashamedly personal, many of these poems invite the reader to a private place, a fragile internal life, which teems with doubt and hope, rather than resolution or assurance. In a subcutaneous, rueful tribute to his mother the poet acknowledges his embarrassment and duplicity, not without harm to his self-esteem:

> She never looked like other boys' mums.
> No one ever looked without looking again
> At the pink kameez and balloon'd bottoms,

> mustard-oiled trail of hair, brocaded pink
> sandals and the smell of curry. That's why
> I'd bin the letters about Parents' Evenings...
>   – 'IN A WHITE TOWN'

Any adolescence contains mixtures of guilt and humiliation, whirlpools of cowardice and secrecy. This poem delves into the ignoble ordeal, as well as catching the bewildered loneliness of this stranded woman:

> two of us alone, she'd duck at my stuttered Punjabi,
> laughing, she'd say I was a gora, I'd only be freed
> by a bride from India who would double as her saathi.

'Saathi' is a lifelong female companion, a dream of home and belonging; Nagra's words do their best to fill a vacancy made all the more poignant by her ageing, by his incomplete adulthood:

> Nowadays, when I visit, when she hovers upward,
> hobbling towards me to kiss my forehead
> as she once used to, I wish I could fall forward.

I have made the volume sound too sombre; it is magnificently serious, but also jam-packed with chuckles and joy. In other words, this Indian in England is not a victim who whines or yearns for some fictional, snatched homeland; he carves out settlement in his own flesh and blood, in the streets where he lives and works. Take, for example, the carnival splendour of 'Our Town with the Whole of India!':

> Our Sunrise Radio with its lip sync of Bollywood lovers
> pumping through the rows of emporium cubby holes
> whilst bhangra beats slam where the hagglers roar
> at the pulled-up back-of-the-lorry cut-price stalls.

Then again:

> Our cafés with the brickwork trays of saffron sweets,
> brass woks frying flamingo-pink syrup-tunnelled
> jalebis networking crustily into their familied clumps.

Again:

> A Somali cab joint, been there for ever, with smiley
> guitar licks where reggae played before Caribbeans
> disappeared, where years before Teddy Boys jived.

What a party! Better by far than the Hounslow High Street of my own, lace-curtained childhood, and yet it's the same place, wonderfully transformed; I think my grandmother might well have approved, lifted her skirt a little.

Even the stereotype confinement of the open-all-hours corner shop becomes an exotic tryst, with a *mis-en-scène* of stale bread, half-price window signs and chocolate bars. A covert revolution unfolds upstairs:

> I run just one ov my daddy's shops
> From 9 o'clock to 9 o'clock
> and he vunt me not to hav a break
> but ven nobody in, I do di lock –

cos up di stairs is my newly bride
vee share in chapatti
vee share in di chutney
after vee hav made luv
like vee rowing through Putney...
                    – 'SINGH SONG!'

That glance at the Varsity Eights on the Thames exemplifies the subtlety and pride of this entire collection The legacy is in the legerdemain.

I very much dislike the cover of my edition of this book. It has a discount store frieze – squeegee mops, potties, ironing boards, plastic carnations. And Daljit's name is splashed in a neo-Sanskrit typeface. Cheap, reductive, almost as if it's not a real Faber text, that restrained, vaticinative house of Eliot, Stevens, Auden, Plath, Heaney. This writer belongs in that company and has much more yet to say; could even go some way to restoring its reputation for innovation and excellence. No facile categories here, no resort for the bigot, the fanatic or the gaping chasm of the 'open mind'. The poet as an individual voice, raised in public:

i have been sitting here
recording myself telling on myself

whatever voice i put on
i know i'm heading for bother

mostly the confessions
i play back to myself

inside my bad-weathered room
are so unrewarding

i may have to go
back into hiding
                    – 'INFORMANT'

You should hear the man read aloud, without a microphone. He brushes away the cobwebs, is at once spiritual and irreverent, crafty and spontaneous. You will not forget what you may not choose to hear.

Fred Johnston

OVER-COOKED GOOSE

Ed. by John Ennis, Randall Maggs and Stephanie McKenzie, *The Echoing Years: An Anthology of Poetry from Canada and Ireland* (The Centre for Newfoundland and Labrador Studies, School of Humanities Publications, Waterford Institute of Technology, 2007), €35 / Canadian $50.

Size matters. A book that weighs in at more than one-and-a-half kilos, the weight of a Makita compact cordless drill or a smallish Yorkshire Terrier, had better say something. Number three in a trilogy of Newfoundland-Ireland concoctions – I contributed to an earlier one – this is the biggest, boldest, most grab-ass of them all. It is to poetry anthologies what one of Saddam Hussein's palaces is to architecture. Ironic, when one recalls that the word 'anthology' derives from the Greek for a bunch of flowers.

Ostensibly a meeting of poetic minds from Canada and Ireland, it does its duty in providing sanctuary to the critically disinherited as well as passing praise for the deserving; it perpetuates myths and allows publishers to parade their stars, even those that are fading. It lists as Irish poets who are not Irish: Oritsegbemi Emmanuel Jakpa is Nigerian, on the MA Creative Writing programme at Waterford Institute of Technology, and Samantha Thomas, on the same course in Waterford, is Caribbean-American. Grace Wells is a Londoner. Nonetheless, their inclusion indicates the slowly changing patterns of poetry produced in Ireland, and this pattern will produce new definitions.

It's left to the French editors, Dominique Gaucher and Jean-Pierre Pelletier, utterly ignored on the cover, to speak directly: 'L'équipe se sentait en terrain moins solide concernant la poésie qu'ils qualifiaient de *canadienne-française...*' The French intro is also interesting, touching upon the development of Québecoise literature and the influences of American 'counter-culture'.

The anthology wears laudatory jacket blurbs for one of its earlier incarnations and for itself sewn by poets who have work included in it; Thomas McCarthy and Bernard O'Donoghue, for instance. Bernard O'Donoghue speaks, no doubt straight-faced, of 'the wonderful serendipity' of which he is a part. It allows a brace of Irish poets to call themselves translators, some of whom have merely reworked poems from provided translated *cribs* – a practice which, as a modest translator, I find insulting, and which should be argued in earnest by the Irish Translators' Association. Unless Bernard O'Donoghue competently knows Czech and can translate Czech poetry *sans* crib; Theo Dorgan Slovene, Patrick Cotter Estonian (the list goes on), then they are not translators of the works in those languages mentioned in 'Notes on Contributors' and cannot be listed as such. Clearly the poetry 'translation' project initiated during Cork's European Capital of Culture époque has been given free rein here, along with, to a more modest degree, Waterford Tech's Creative Writing Course.

One feels there was something a tad lazy about the compiling of the book. Were easy solutions sought? And why were the names of the original non-Irish authors highlighted in big typeface in the Irish index and their Irish re-interpreters given tiny type beneath them? Oddly, a real translator, Pearse Hutchinson, gets a look-in with only one of his own Irish-language poems, and that translated by Gréagóir Ó Dúill.

Because one may be rendered cautious, let's say, over the Irish selections here, one may be reasonably cautious over the rest; it's not difficult to speculate, for instance, that having publishers of poetry as advisors on an anthology can have a prejudicial influence on the content.

So what is this verbal gridlock about? Ultimately, it's unclear. Foras na Gaeilge had a toe in it all, as did The Ireland Newfoundland Partnership: one anthology would have been enough, three in five years is over-cooking a tender goose, surely. *The Backyards of Heaven: Contemporary Poetry from Ireland and Newfoundland and Labrador*, came out in 2003, followed by *However Blow the Winds: Poetry and Song from Newfoundland and Labrador and Ireland* in 2004. For this book to work it might have shown us plain an Irish poetry that had changed, metamorphosed, altered; it cannot do that because the conservative nature of Irish poetic voice and the peri-institutionalised nature of its publishing and promoting worlds have cauterised potential development. The presence of the late Traveller poet and songstress Ellie Carr is a flicker of light in the dim scullery of the Irish section's predictability. For the matter of that, we could have done with less Michael Longley and more the innovative Maurice Scully; Scully's work, shamefully absent here, would have run well alongside Canadian poet bpNichol's 'St. Anzas VIII':

> sh.together
> quietness the scream, anguish anyway. anxiety
> lived with. terror. t's error &
> s's in – in everything...

Whereas the Canadians are unafraid of the challenge of experimental writers, this is a phobia we have yet to overcome. The Irish section by and large runs the risk of merely reinforcing whole sets of prejudices and preconceptions. Attempting to create a contemporary poetic pantheon, we appear to have thrown up a ramshackle bamboo temple to our own determined self-absorption.

It is the French-language poets to whom we turn to look for other types of innovation; here we have Louise Dupré's beautiful untitled sequence of prose-poetry: 'Tout est possible à l'ombre des jardins, dans la luxe / de leurs parfums . . .' Then there's Jean-Marc Desgent's darkly murmurring, ominous, 'Les premiers paysages':

> Ici, même s'il y avait la disparition
> des bêtes et des filles,
> la grande déportation
> des choses et des garçons,
> les destructions de langues et d'âmes...

French-language poetry, be it from Canada or mainland France, has not allowed itself to be stripped of a clear, defined lyric sense, even when the subject matter is dark. Thus can Desgent link 'languages' and 'spirit / souls'. There seems to be something about writing contemporary poetry in English that almost by default threatens its lyrical possibilities. The French language retains its music in its sounds, so many of which are created in nasal cavities, as if the skull itself were a musical instrument; contemporary English merely turns the mouth into a typewriter.

For all the mass of this curiously weightless anthology, for this reviewer the magic rested with a few French-language poems. Its use might be to make us look at how unchanging, unthreatening, so much modern Irish poetry (but not all, thankfully) can be, and how circumscribed by a need to conform and leave unrocked the very boats poetry was launched to rock. Irish poetry will be changed utterly when the sons and daughters of immigrants to this country begin to write from a fusion of their inherited and acquired cultures. There is irony here, given that we are a two-tongued, two-cultured nation as it is. But then might we see a poetry that does not merely talk to – or against – itself.

Maria Johnston

HUMAN VOICES

Bernard O'Donoghue, *Selected Poems* (Faber and Faber, 2008) £12.99.
Julie O'Callaghan, *Tell Me This is Normal: New and Selected Poems* (Bloodaxe
Books, 2008) £8.95.

Bernard O'Donoghue's recently published *Selected Poems*, opens with the
breathtaking 'A Nun Takes the Veil', the title of which echoes G M
Hopkins's entrancing, escapist monologue 'Heaven-Haven: A Nun Takes
the Veil'. This equally evocative monologue, voiced by an ageing Irish
nun, is a delicately-detailed remembrance of her leaving home for the
cloistered life, delivered without sentiment, as the heightened moment is
recaptured in all its luminous vibrancy:

> That morning early I ran through briars
> To catch the calves that were bound for market.
> I stopped the once, to watch the sun
> Rising over Doolin across the water.
>
> The calves were tethered outside the house
> While I had my breakfast: the last one at home
> For forty years. I had what I wanted (they said
> I could), so we'd loaf bread and Marie biscuits.

O'Donoghue, as a poet and scholar who is deeply attentive to formal
artistry – the sophisticated European poetry of the troubadours and the
Minnesänger is exemplary for him – has commented on how his poems
often have a 'medieval shape' and, to my mind, many of the elements
that Edwin Morgan admired in Old English poetry (and in Ezra Pound's
early Cantos) – alliteration, four-stressed lines, falling rhythms – are
employed here to deliberate effect. The four-stress Anglo-Saxon line of
two separate, balanced halves ('I stopped the once, to watch the sun') is
in harmony with the halting flow of the speaker's natural speech pattern
while the falling cadences of end-words such as 'homeward' and
'mainland' create a sense of a dying music. The poet's natural feeling for
sound and syntax has the poem open with 'that morning early' – instead
of the more conventional 'early that morning' – the stress falling on
'morning' to create an iambic swing. Another pivotal word that anchors
two of the line-ends is 'home' in a poem that chronicles the loss of a
home, of a family and the relinquishment of worldliness. Throughout

this moving poem of propulsive movement, present participles proliferate – 'rising', 'watching', 'seeing' – and significantly, the word 'driving' is repeated, with 'the puffins driving homeward' and her last sight of her father 'Driving cattle to Ballyvaughan'. While most of the stanzas are enclosed within full-stops (indicative, perhaps, of the speaker's circumscribed expressivity) at certain, crucial points – where the word 'driving' occurs – the words are themselves driven across the white space of the stanza-break. This repeated 'driving' action propels the poem into the moment of epiphany that engages the final two stanzas:

> I saw a car for the first time ever,
> Hardly seeing it before it vanished.
> I couldn't believe it, and I stood up looking
> To where I could hear its noise departing
>
> But it was only a glimpse. That night in the convent
> The sisters spoilt me, but I couldn't forget
> The morning's vision, and I fell asleep
> With the engine humming through the open window.

The fresh exhilaration that haunts these concluding stanzas makes for a poem that is utterly unforgettable, just as 'that morning' has remained bright and clear in the speaker's memory, the car engine 'humming' into the continuous present. The poem itself is a vehicle, transporting us across the boundless expanse of the past. It is the poet's attentiveness to the colloquial idiom, in the phrase 'I couldn't believe it', that subtly conveys deeper revelations to the reader as, ironically, the speaker, who has committed herself to a life of faith, of belief in God, *couldn't believe* the man-made motor car that she saw with her own eyes. As this is the only 'vision' that graces her life, the poem ends with the pull of the secular, validating the things of this world that are common to us and yet still wondrous. O'Donoghue in his searching, unobtrusive way eschews any final judgment allowing the speaker's own words to communicate, thus making possible an endlessly layered meditation on human existence. In all of this, one is reminded of Eamon Grennan's memorable description of the 'power of the telling voice' in the work of John McGahern; its ability 'to anchor the unsteady universe of consciousness and moral complexity in the simple, concrete data of ordinary life.'

As is evident, O'Donoghue's poetry captures the rubato of everyday human utterance and makes from it its own instinctive, compulsive music. His ear for the rhythms and cadences of speech – and for the silences, heart-heavy, between the notes – is pitch-perfect. In ' "Dogs, Would you Live For Ever?" ' one is reminded once more of the narrative style of

McGahern's work and, to quote Grennan again, its 'impeccably caught and exactly registered (to often devastatingly painful or comic effect) dialogue.' Thus:

> Crying, she says 'This is the worst now.'
> I say 'Of course it's not.
> You did as much for children
> Often enough.'
>
> But of course it was: the scene
> Comes back, untriggered, more
> Rather than less often,
> Oddly enough.
>
> I'd prefer you to wait outside.

As the stark 'scene' unfolds the reader is drawn in, forced to stand in the doorway and bear witness. Firstly, there is the graphic, sustained focus on the dying woman's abject body as she defecates – her arched back is likened to 'white fish / That has been too long in the fridge, / Greyed at the spine-bones' – broken only by the accompanying snatch of conversation that the reader guiltily overhears. The mastery of the poem's execution is in this verbal exchange between the two. The speaker's mode of articulation reveals what his words cannot, that he is mindless with inexpressible grief, his familiar, clumsy clichés – 'as the saying is', 'oddly enough' – serving only to amplify the staggering emotion. Also illuminated in this brief, deftly-realised exchange are the lies and half-truths that we hold to at dissonant moments of failure. The prohibitive final line, uttered by we know not who, or to whom, implicates the reader directly; we are only permitted limited access, limited knowledge. These are poems that do not draw attention to themselves; they border on silence, darkness, and draw us in with the thing half-said, with what is left unspoken. One is reminded of James Joyce's *Dubliners* – Joyce is an important precursor for O'Donoghue as he was for McGahern – and his employment of the ellipsis to signify paralysis. O'Donoghue's best work registers the fragile, fragmented reality of human experience and voices the inescapable uncertainties of existence. It is O'Donoghue's narrative technique that makes so many of the poems here so lasting; the reader cannot look away as 'the scene comes back, untriggered.'

A similar mastery of delivery is there in 'Ter Conatus' and its grim, painstaking etching of emotional paralysis between a man and his dying sister. The title points to Virgil's *Aeneid* and Aeneas's meeting with the ghost of his father in the underworld: 'Thrice he tried there to throw his arms around his neck, thrice the vision eluded his arms'. This heart-breaking, abortive triple-attempt is subtly taken up in the poem: '"D'you want a hand?" he asked, / / Taking a step towards her. "I can manage," / She answered, feeling for the stairs. / Three times, like that, he tried to reach her.' In this, as in so many of O'Donoghue's quiet masterpieces, an everyday circumstance is revealed to contain the everywhere tragedies of human existence in poems that speak from the page. As well as the artistry of McGahern, one is reminded too of Robert Frost's dramatic monologues and dialogues. One of O'Donoghue's outstanding elegies, 'Any Last Requests', has the poet-as-speaker ostensibly engaged in his English life as a dear friend is being buried in Co Cork: 'I'm busy brushing wood preservative / into my English garden fence' he addresses the dead man, in lines that seem to demand as response the incriminating words from Frost's 'Home Burial': 'Three foggy mornings and one rainy day / Will rot the best birch fence a man can build.' Obsolescence is the dominant theme throughout O'Donoghue's poetry. Allen Ginsberg dismissed 'Home Burial' as a 'coupla squares yakking' but in Frost, as in O'Donoghue, it is in these commonplace human exchanges that the universal themes of existence are exposed.

Although O'Donoghue may be classified as an Irish émigré poet, he is refreshingly without the anxieties and hang-ups of the exiled, displaced expatriate, revelling instead in his freedom to inhabit more than one place: 'It's good to have two places. Two perspectives', he has commented. Like McGahern, he may be seen to draw often on a particular place – the rural world of his childhood – but this becomes universal and vast in its scope. 'The past is a foreign country', O'Donoghue has quoted approvingly and this is central to an understanding of his long view, one that extends back to the beginnings of poetry itself. O'Donoghue is not only steeped in the Irish traditions of his native Cork but has long been committed to the study of old and middle English as a teacher of medieval literature at Oxford University. His anthology *The Courtly Love Tradition* (1982) brought together his own translations of medieval poetry from French, German, Italian, Georgian and Arabic. Part of the delight of reading him is the understanding that emerges of the continuity of the past into the present, of other traditions and the connections that may be traced between these. With characteristic insight he has comment-ed on how 'connected' classical Irish Bardic poetry and Old English in fact are. Similarly, Pound heard the rhythms of a Gaelic folk song replicated in *Beowulf*. One of the lamentable omissions from this *Selected* is the love poem 'Love's Medium' from *Outliving* (2003) which draws on the strange, shadowy medieval love lament *Wulf and Eadwacer*.

Seamus Heaney has described the impact of reading, in a poem by John Crowe Ransom, the line 'Sweet ladies, long may ye bloom, and toughly I hope ye may thole' thus; 'my heart lifted again, the world widened, something was furthered.' O'Donoghue is a poet who widens the world for us and who makes possible a deeper understanding of the plurality and complexities of all human experience. His 'ideal' of the short poem is as he has said 'the kind of "wisdom" poetry represented by the Old English elegy' and like the poets of *The Wanderer* and *The Seafarer* he is, to my mind, similarly concerned with the profound ambiguities of human experience and with the life of the mind. For O'Donoghue the ideal poem is 'a mixture of universal emotion ("Where have the joys of company gone? Alas! The Bright cup!") and the power of the half-stated.' It seems appropriate that the lines quoted here by O'Donoghue from *The Wanderer* are spoken by one who 'ponders wisely in his mind / and goes over this life in its darkness and its origins / with insight of heart.' O'Donoghue's work communicates the importance of humility in the face of an unknowable universe and the centrality to this of 'love and whim and irrational attachment' ('Shells of Galice').

Perhaps surprisingly, much of which has been said here of O'Donoghue may be repeated for O'Callaghan – surprising as O'Callaghan's poetry is usually deemed 'light-verse'. Kingsley Amis, expounding on the rigorous skill that the writing of successful 'light verse' demands, likened the 'light verse' poet to a juggler, the writer of 'high verse' to a concert pianist, thus: 'A concert pianist is allowed a wrong note here and there: a juggler is not allowed to drop a plate.' It is rare that O'Callaghan drops a plate – all the more of a feat when one considers that all of her super-sized plates are food-laden (she has been called the 'true laureate of tucker and nosh') – or yet sounds a wrong note. Like O'Donoghue, O'Callaghan may be classified as an émigré writer – she has lived all of her adult life outside her native America, moving to Ireland at the age of twenty – yet it is this double perspective and the imaginative resource it makes available that enables a poetry that is original, fresh and engaging. O'Callaghan was born in Chicago in 1954 – or 'Chicawgo' as she more accurately transcribes its pronunciation – and the brash soundscape and distinctive character of that city's disorderly human life, its slang and street talk, is captured throughout many of these lively performance pieces. One is reminded of G K Chesterton's belief that 'the one stream of poetry which is constantly flowing is slang'. Indeed, the title of the selection, with its definitively American, over-the-top wail, 'Tell me this is normal', signals the work's grounding in the vernacular, in the registers and inflections of American speech. The performative aspect is central; O'Callaghan excels in the dramatic monologue with an ear as keen as O'Donoghue's even as she works in a very different style. Indeed, Ginsberg's phrase 'coupla squares yakking' comes to mind again as one listens in on a poetry that is full of yap, chit-chat and all the noisy bustle of humanity as it consumes and is consumed. The distinctive art work of John Register has adorned the cover of more than one of O'Callaghan's volumes, with pictures that portray the contemporary city as a site of human isolation. As Register has explained; 'in my pictures, I think you, the viewer, become the isolated one.' Underlying many of O'Callaghan's dramatic monologues and dialogues there is, to my mind, an unshakeable sense of the isolate human voice and the void of white space that surrounds its yowls and yawps.

Like O'Donoghue, O'Callaghan is too shrewd and knowing to look back with simplistic nostalgia to her homeland. Indeed, her perceptive poem 'The Great Blasket Island' is a cool, spunky ticking-off to those who would self-indulgently shed tears over the loss of a home-place: 'Listen, mister, most of us cry sooner or later / over a Great Blasket Island of our own.' To my mind her 'native' city seems as endlessly foreign and baffling to her as her adopted country. After all, this is a poet who has remarked that 'the most important attribute needed for poetry is a sense of how odd it is to be a humanoid. If you don't wake up each morning on a foreign planet, you can forget poetry as a pastime.' The monologue 'Local Man Tells of Native City', spoken by a garrulous mid-Westerner who has never ventured far from his front door, is a sharp, sparkling parody of regionalism and native values:

> Well, it's my kinda town for one.
> Ya got yer Cubs, White Sox, Bears and Black Hawks
> and as for that faggoty game they play
> over there in Europe
> – kick the ball – well I tell ya,
> we got that one too
> only I ain't gonna brag about it, see?

The speaker concludes his paean to Chicago with two lines that encapsulate his character exactly as he repeats the home-spun rhymes of Frank Sinatra's 'My Kind of Town': 'Each time I roam Chicago keeps calling me home. / It's the one town that won't let you down.' O'Callaghan has the skill of a ventriloquist – in other poems throughout she assumes the voice of a Japanese court-lady, a Degas dancer, a yuppie – and this range of voices and modes of expression makes for a poetry of bracing variety. O'Callaghan is thoroughly unpretentious. There is none of the usual, cringe-inducing self-indulgence and trite pseudo-insights of the narcissistic poet-as-speaker that one encounters in so much of the poetry that draws on modern, contemporary experience in a hip bid for 'honesty'. We see very little of the person behind the poet in this play of voices and character pieces. O'Callaghan, although she confronts human suffering in her poems, does not attempt to make any grand pronouncements or large-scale comparisons. The title poem of her collection *No Can Do*, is a winningly ballsy monologue spoken by a cancer-sufferer and thoroughly without self-pity:

> Chip is like:
> 'How come you don't want to
> to go out anyplace?'
>
> I'm this huge moose
> with no hair,
> a cheapo wig and cancer.
> And I'm supposed to go
> and eat a Seafood Platter?
> No can do.

Tellingly, the 'cancer' comes last in her list of self-defining attributes. Another poem, titled 'Auschwitz', defies expectations as it is set in what is now the museum of the concentration camp. Spoken by a mouthy tourist, it ends with her bawling out her snapshot-obsessed travel companion, Brad, as he insists on posing for another photograph: 'You're gonna be murdered if you don't get out / of that rotten old gas oven.' This, to me, reveals more about the condition of humanity than many other serious poems on the subject have.

Another highlight is the elegy for her father. As this assemblage of 'sketches' makes clear – this elegy is not to be an over-blown epic – a life can only be sketched tentatively in random images that are true to the processes of memory and that resist the order of artful, artificial patterns. Yet the artistry lies in the way that these vignettes of the most stubbornly ordinary moments from her father's last days engage the reader to the end. The elegist addresses her dead father in a poem that momentarily restores him to life only for him to die again, over and again, through the workings of words and memory:

> you still laughed at Seinfeld
> and watered your plants
> and read *The New Yorker*
> and the Tuesday Science section
> OK, it hurt a lot
> and you said you'd never wear
> your bike helmet again
> but dying was easier
> than I'd thought...
>   – 'Sketches for an Elegy'

O'Callaghan's qualities as a poet are such that her 'light verse' is worth far more than this diminutive term suggests. At her best, she revitalises poetic language and assaults the dulled, modern ear, in poems that, with their bold demotic diversity, expand our sense of how poetry can speak and where it may be found. She is a poet who registers all the untidy activity of human life as it is: awful but cheerful, or, to use the title of one of her new poems, infinitely 'Scary'.

Proinsias Ó Drisceoil

FRACTURED YET VIBRANT

Meg Bateman, *Soirbheas* (Polygon, 2007), £9.99.
Maoilios Caimbeul, *Breac-A'-Mhuiltein* (*Spéir Dhroim an Ronnaigh*)
(Coiscéim, 2007), €15.
Rody Gorman, *Zonda? Khamsin? Sharaav? Camanchaca?* (Leabhraichean
Beaga, Inbhir Nis, 2006), £6.
Rob MacIlleChiar, *Aiteachadh* (diehard at the Callander Press, 2007), £3.
Ed. by Rody Gorman, *An Guth 5* (Coiscéim, 2008), €10.

In the final poem of *Soirbheas* ('Envoi'), Meg Bateman gives voice to her
estrangement from the translated version of one of her Gaelic originals
as she came on it in an anthology of love poems, where it appears in a
section on the theme of eternal commitment. The fact that the 'eternal
commitment' of the poem had really only lasted for three weeks
prompts her to warn the reader 'that reality and poetic truth are not the
same' ('nach ionann firinn na beatha is firinn na bàrdachd'). But even
more importantly the translation seemed alienated from the literary and
linguistic influences at work on the Gaelic original:

> gun iomradh fiù 's gum b'i a' Gàidhlig
> a' bhean-ghlùine 'dhaibh no am bogha.

> (with no mention that Gaelic
> was either the midwife or the bow).

However the counter-argument could be made that each and every one
of her poems is a work of translation, translations into poetry of a raw
life of which the reader, necessarily concentrating on the poetry, can
know little. Not that these poems are self-ironising essays in detachment;
rather are they poems of metaphysical engagement expressing an
'affirming light', a hard-won grace in the face of struggle, loss and
frustration: 'ár míshuaimhneas síoraí' ('our enduring unease'), in Eoghan
Ó Tuairisc's memorable phrase from 'Aifreann na Marbh'. Here evasion
and self-deceit are confronted in a search for significant truth through
poems that explore relationship with lovers, parents, a child, other
women and neighbours.

In Bateman's poems what lovers have in common is the distance
between them:

Tha mi aonaranach nad leabaidh
do ghàirdeanan mun cuairt orm
trom leis an deoch…

ach mus cadail thu
nach faighnich thu, "Dè do shaoghal?"

(I am lonely in your bed,
the arms encircling me
heavy with drink…

but before you sleep
won't you ask me how I am?)

        – 'GUM FAICTE SLÀN MI'

In a rewrite of Somhairle Mac Gill-Eain's well-known poem, 'Corra-Ghritheach' ('Heron'), she is the fish for which the heron waits:

Is mi reòite ri do thaobh
a' feitheamh ach an till do mhiann…

(So I am frozen at your side
waiting for your desire to return…)

Bateman is an authority on medieval poetry (something which suggests a possible comparison with Bernard O'Donoghue): thus early Irish lyric poetry and medieval religious poetry are dominant influences. The result is a well-formed coherent poem that relies entirely on contemporary Gaelic with no resort to neologism, antiquated vocabulary or strained syntax. The influence of the religious poetry may have abetted the search by the *persona* of the poems for ideal relationships, for a modern equivalent to the saints and holy family of medieval verse: thus a desire for complete selfhood strains against the quotidian, issuing in self-doubt, confusion and brokenness. Her recollection of Christmas dinners ('Biadh na Nollaige') is marred by:

… acras airson Nollaigean eile –
agus Nollaigean nach robh riamh ann –
acras airson fhaclan òrdha
a bhuachailleadh dhan aon chrò sinn.

(… a hunger for other Christmases
and Christmases that had never been –
a hunger for golden words
that would herd us into the one fold.)

If there is reconciliation to self and the lived life it comes through 'an rèite a dh'ionnsaicheas bròn', 'the peace taught by grief' ('Dadaidh'). The limitations observed by Bateman in the translations (by herself) of the Gaelic original should not obscure the fact that her English versions are poems in themselves and non-readers of Gaelic will find in *Soirbheas* poems to match those written in either language over recent years.

Breac-A'-Mhuiltein (Spéir Dhroim an Ronnaigh) draws on five published collections by Maoilios Caimbeul, as well as on more recent work, to give a 339-page selected poems. Whereas Bateman translates her own work into English, Caimbeul's preference is for translation within the Gaelic family: here, fellow-poet Rody Gorman renders the poems into Irish. While Bateman offers translations that can vary the originals in response to the poetic requirements of her English versions, Gorman stays with the text of the original poems with the result that his translations shadow the originals more precisely than do Bateman's.

Contrary to what might be assumed, translation from Scottish Gaelic into Irish Gaelic is a more intricate task than translation of the same poems into English. Problems arise when a word or phrase in Scottish Gaelic exists, perhaps in mutated form, in Irish dictionaries but is not in general use in the spoken language: if too many such words and phrases appear in the Irish version the resulting poems can seem stilted and antiquarian; if completely ignored the translation may appear to be oblivious to the common lexical inheritance. Where, for instance, Caimbeul's poem 'A' Càradh an Rathaid' includes the line 'an t-aon a dhèanadh feum', Gorman might have been expected to give something like 'an t-aon a dhéanfadh feidhm', thus recycling Caimbeul's word usage. Instead he gives 'an t-aon cheann a dhéanfadh beart', which employs a different vocabulary but conveys Caimbeul's meaning with much greater clarity.

Caimbeul is a poet of observation and his poems have a presentness and live sensitivity that is combined with an assured use of his native Staffan Gaelic to give poems in a developed personal style. His art is more oblique, far less confessional than Bateman's; his worldview is at once local and international, as in 'Dihaoine 3.3.2000':

> Ann am Mozambique
> tuiltean uabhasach. Rugadh
> leanabh ann an craoibh...
>
> Bho seo a-mach bidh
> na craobhan a'sgiamhail rium
> nuair bhios e sileadh.

(I Mozambique
tuilte uafásacha. Rugadh
leanbh i gcrann...

Uaidh seo amach beidh
na crainn ag gol orm
nuair a bhíonn sé ag sileadh.)

Liam Prút ('Do Rody Gorman') has compared the productivity of Rody
Gorman to the man who could not stop his salt mill and so filled the sea
with salt. 'Scanraíonn do bhisiúlacht mé' ('your productivity scares me')
says Prút and, certainly, Gorman's engagement with Gaelic poetry, both
Scottish and Irish, has been an outstanding and hugely energising feature
of recent decades.

   Zonda? Khamsin? Sharaav? Camanchaca? derives its puzzling title from
an attempt by Gorman to imagine what the names given to the wind 'A
bha sèideach oirre bho Mhòrair' ('blowing from Morar') might have been
'Nuair nach robh Mòrair ann' ('when Morar did not exist'). This is in line
with Gorman's ceaseless exploration of words, their use and meaning.
'Fonn', the initial word of the title 'Fonn agus Fògradh', provides in itself
sufficient semantic range for Gorman to go immediately to play with its
multiple meanings. 'Fonn' is given in Mark's *Gaelic-English Dictionary* as
'airs, descant, tone, tune', but 'soil, sod under one's feet' might also have
been given. Gorman utilises all of these meanings in a poem in which he
parallels his own years as a Dubliner in Scotland with the exile of Colm
Cille. Unlike Colm Cille, his is not an irreversible exile and his native sod
remains solid beneath his feet:

   Bidh fàd mo dhùthchais fhèin
   Gu sìorraidh fo mo chois.

Gorman's poetry is marked by great clarity of image and always seeks to
communicate crisply and clearly; the strongest influence is probably the
brevity and vividness of William Carlos Williams. Connections between
places are also important, between the Blasket Islands and Barra, for
instance, in the poem 'Tarraing' where the title ('Pull') indicates, perhaps,
their shared identification with rowing and the sea. In seeking to connect
he also seeks to domesticate: in his poem 'My Lai' that event and those
of the same period are Gaelicised, domesticated and granted an
historical status by the poet who wonders what Gaelic name the year
might have been given:

Bliadhna 'n t-Sneachda Bhuidhe
No Bliadhna 'n Earraich Dhuibh...

(The Year of the Yellow Snow or the Year of the Black Spring...)

Gorman is a poet of the brief lyric but in 'A' Bheinn Fhuar' he writes a
longer poem, drawing heavily on eastern poetry for imagery of self-exile,
the significant and essential. Similarly in 'Táladh' ('Attraction' / 'Draw') he
recalls an Islay man from whom he heard what was neither a song nor a
verse but:

.....'S e bh'ann
Ach an turram sin
Is tàladh na bruinne.

(It is that murmur which is the pull of the womb.)

Gorman's 'bodach' (oldman, oldster) haunts the collection. In 'Brodadh'
he describes how every morning after he rises he uses a fork to open a tin
of cat food:

'S ann a tha mi air m'ais
Anns a' mhòine còmhla ris a' bhodach...

(I am back on the bog with the old man...)

The Scottish Gaelic of this collection is untranslated. (Any attempt at
translation is likely to involve an element of misrepresentation: the
unpoetic literal translations given in this review are the reviewer's own.)
Taken together with collections such as his largely Irish Gaelic collection
An Duilleog agus an Crotal (Coiscéim, 2004) or his other untranslated
Scottish Gaelic collection, *Eadar Fiaradh is Balbh* (diehard at the Callander
Press, 2007), this collection gives us one of the most recognisable voices
in modern Gaelic poetry.
    Rob MacIlleChiar is a Gaelic learner, a native of Argyll, now living in
Skye, where Gorman's concision has been a clear influence on his art.
Aiteachadh (*Cultivation / Agriculture / Settlement*) includes translations from
Rilke, Bashō and others as well as a series derived from native North
American poetry. However the closest formal parallel is with the poetry
in Irish of Gabriel Rosenstock, although no direct acquaintance with
Rosenstock's work is apparent. Like Rosenstock, many of MacIlleChiar's
poems are haikus or close cousins of same. Nature poems predominate
and the brevity of these allows full expression to his gift for visual

precision and the observation of transience. His style is experimental, polished and wrought and as the collection is untranslated (part of a series from this publisher) similar reservations about translation must be expressed as in the case of Gorman:

> Uisge a' lìonadh
> làrach-chasan ùr
> air an t-seann slighe.

> (Rain filling a new footprint on the old pathway.)

The final series of poems is titled 'Bho Ameireagaidh A Tuath' (From North America) and as well as the Native Indian series it includes two prose poems of some power. One of these is titled 'Orain Choiseachd' and gives voice to the importance of travel to his poetry:

> Tha tiodhlac an òranaiche na thiodhlac an rathaid.

> (The poet's gift is the gift for the road.)

An Guth founded and edited by Rody Gorman is now in its fifth year. This remarkable project (273 pages long in the current edition) comprises original work by poets writing in Irish, Scottish Gaelic and Manx. Many poems are presented in both their original form and in the form of translations into the alternative language form. Thus, for instance, the Scottish Gaelic poem 'The e Doirbh Smaoineachadh Uaireannan' by Murchadh Dòmhnallach is accompanied by an Irish translation, made by the editor, 'Is Deacair Smaoineamh Scaití'. Other poems allow readers who are only proficient in one form of Gaelic to read poems written in the other form by providing a short vocabulary underneath the poem.

Bateman, Caimbeul and MacIlleChiar all contribute but the overwhelming majority of contributors are from Ireland: perhaps the ubiquity of English-language translations in Scottish Gaelic gives the poets concerned an access to the English-speaking world which poets published in untranslated Irish are denied. Thus the common Gaelic dimension developed by *An Guth* allows poets writing in Irish some measure of international recognition, something they are far less likely to achieve than are their English-language contemporaries in Ireland.

In an era when cross-cultural interpretation is at the core of cultural life, *An Guth* is a project of outstanding relevance and importance in the repossession and re-imagination of a fractured yet vibrant heritage.

Michael O'Loughlin

HYPHENATED PEOPLE

Ian Duhig, *The Speed Of Dark* (Picador Poetry, 2007), £8.99.

With his first four collections Duhig established himself as one of the most original and brilliant (in every sense of the word) poets of his time. Tony Harrison without the hang-ups, Geoffrey Hill with a sense of humour. The North of England has evidently rocked his cradle, and no better place. In this new collection he once again pairs linguistic wit with seriousness of purpose, to great effect.

Born in London into an Irish-speaking immigrant family, Duhig always has the Great Shade at his shoulder. His mother recited Yeats to him when he was a child, and in a way Yeats is his true mother tongue. It could not be more apt: if Duhig is not Anglo-Irish, who is? His penchant for formal metres and ballad forms (and content) brings him into a Yeatsian arena, though he is coming from precisely the opposite direction. Larkin rejected Yeats on behalf of English poetry, mumbling about rhetoric and romanticism, but he missed the point. Duhig, like Yeats, is above all a realist, who wants to engage (a dusty word) with reality on as many levels as he can.

The collection opens with a moving and finely-wrought elegy to the Irish-American poet Michael Donaghy, who he later refers to in another poem as 'one of we hyphenated people'. Duhig is drawn to the hyphenated people, which at this stage includes most of us and our children, and one of the most dazzling poems in the book operates in this area. He has already done a famously burlesque version of 'Nineteen Hundred and Nineteen', but in the poem 'Brilliant' he goes even further. Growing up Irish in England during the IRA's bombing campaigns in the 1970s and 1980s, Duhig is highly attuned to the problems faced by the hyphenated communities. He was acquainted in Leeds with one of the 7/7 London bombers, and tries to rework 'Easter 1916' in this context. Typically the poem takes its epigraph from the Kaiser Chiefs: 'Everything in Leeds is Brilliant.'

> I met him one brilliant day
> coming with brilliant faces
> from clinic at number 12a
> on our way to more brilliant places.
> Then, riding a bus into town,
> I sorted the world out with Sid...

[...]

> This bomber's Dad ran a chip shop
> which fried not with dripping but oil;
> on match days he stood on the Kop
> with Sid, now Sidique, from the school...
>   — 'BRILLIANT'

The poem is not completely successful, perhaps inevitably considering the different positions from which Yeats and Duhig are approaching the subject matter, but few poets would have the daring or skill to attempt it.

The centrepiece of this collection is a series of reworkings and versions of the fourteenth-century French text *Le Roman de Fauvel*. Duhig strikes a rich vein here, the broad, medieval yet linguistically precise satire is perfect for his skills, allowing him to swing between high and low culture. The trope of using the Middle Ages as a mirror for our times is not new but has seldom been used in such a virtuoso manner:

> but now your naval empire's wrecked,
> your tongue one Yankee dialect,
> your politics a Trojan horse
> or fig-leaf for her naked force.
> If 'cheval' bore our chivalry,
> our heirs the US Cavalry
> ride helicopters to a fight
> to show their Saracens what's right...
>   — 'FAUVEL'S PROLOGUE'

Colonel Kilgore is hovering nearby, inhaling the smell of napalm in the morning! But despite the high jinks and horse laughs ('What horse's mouth would tell you wrong?'), the satire has a serious intent: there is nothing funny about being ruled by the people we are currently ruled by, some of whom emblematically wear cowboy boots. Like Anthony Cronin in *The End Of The Modern World*, he explores the connections between chivalry and capitalism in its many incarnations.

But whatever the strengths of individual poems, for me one of the great pleasures in reading this book is the strange and playful repetition of phrases and imagery. In one poem he refers to a childhood nickname 'echolally', and his echolalia is obsessive, so that clusters of meaning and imagery begin to emerge like a parallel, more elusive book. For example, in one poem inspired by a Vatican propaganda film seen in childhood, he recalls the white First Communion suit which the little Catholic Giacomo wears. The suit resurfaces a few poems later in Polanski's *Chinatown*, on the back of Jack Nicholson:

> ...the private eye out of his depth,
>
> flawed as Dunaway's iris which he notices too late,
>
> his first suit white enough for a Chinese funeral.
>
> — 'TRAVELLING EXHIBITIONS'

The black-and-white contrast itself is reworked and rehearsed in characteristic fashion. Did you know that the Man in Black's only novel was called *Man In White*? And just offscreen, there are his lines from a poem in *The Lammas Hireling*: '...my brother's whole prison wing, a moving barcode / In the black-and-white striped shirts of Newcastle United'.

In another example of this technique, the phrase 'Give Me Your Hand' keeps recurring, once as 'Da Mihi Manum', invoking an unspoken phrase in Irish. The Irish language is often a ghostly presence in his work:

> Bán also means blankness,
>
> nothing, no tone;
>
> the colour of silence,
>
> snow melted by rain;
>
> for nothing's as fair
>
> as the swan's fatal air,
>
> never heard here,
>
> never heard there.
>
> — 'VARIATIONS'

But English is his language, and his linguistic invention can be matched by few. Once read, phrases like 'their lenses scratched / to frosty webs, to skaters' pediscripts on thin ice' are scratched onto the imagination forever. And has impotent, violent, semi-literate fascism ever been better stuffed and mounted than as 'the provisional wing of the meek'?

No doubt about it, Ian Duhig too is just brilliant.

David Butler

A DAINTY DISH

Paul Muldoon, *When the Pie Was Opened* (American University of Paris, The Cahiers Series No. 8, 2008), £10.

Paul Muldoon's *When the Pie Was Opened* is the eighth chapbook in the Cahiers Series of bilingually set-out translations published by the American University of Paris, which has recently inaugurated a Centre for Writers and Translators in its new Arts Arena. Like fellow Northern Irish poet and near contemporary, Ciaran Carson, with whose linguistic free-for-all Muldoon's post-modernist pyrotechnics have frequently been compared, Muldoon's approach to translation is playful and, at times, devilishly inventive. For the purist, both poets more properly pen 'versions' rather than 'translations', but let that go. The Centre for Writers and Translators has no interest in mere glosses of canonical poems. As the Cahier editor notes, 'the ambition of the series is to make available new explorations in writing, in translating, and in the areas linking these two activities.' For an intervention like *When the Pie Was Opened*, who better than Muldoon to set a linguistic cat among the four and twenty blackbirds?

Irish readers will be familiar with Muldoon's free renderings of the Irish of his friend Nuala Ní Dhomhnaill. Indeed, on occasion, one could be forgiven for taking, say, Muldoon's 'The Language Issue' or 'As for the Quince' as the originals of 'Ceist na Teangan' or 'An Crann', so widely anthologised have they become. Like Carson, Muldoon's approach to language is Joycean in its love of sound, pun, and the layered meaning of words more properly termed polysemy. By rendering O'Dhomhnaill's 'Ceist' as 'Issue', for instance, Muldoon already anticipates the trope of the basket of the infant Moses released upon the Nile's flood. In the present collection, Muldoon's language interests delve back into the older tongues of the British Isles. He tackles not only the anonymous song 'An Spailpín Fánach', but Ovid's 'Amores 1.5', Dafydd ap Gwilym's 'Y Gal' from the medieval Welsh, and the anonymous Anglo-Saxon poem 'Wulf and Eadwacer'.

In keeping with his declared intention to 'give some sense of the rollicking spirit of the original', Muldoon shows a rare lightness of touch in his rendering of 'An Spailpín Fánach' as 'The Wandering Navvy'. On this occasion, he eschews his instinctive verbal trickery to capture well the 'come-all-ye' rhythm and register of the original:

No more to Cashel I'll repair
To sell myself at auction
Nor loiter at a hiring fair,
A roadside wall my station.
When a gentleman on his high horse
Asks if I'm hired already,
'One fine day,' says I, 'You'll finish the course
Behind the Irish navvy.'

Muldoon has a superb ear for cadence, and his inventive approach to rhyme is legendary. The Irish original depends on end-rhyme assonance for much of its loose structural unity, a stratagem Muldoon's English is very sensitive to. Thus the Irish sequence 'shláinte / sráide / híreálta / Fánach / Cháile / le h-áireamh / laidir / Ó Dálaigh' becomes, in 'The Wandering Navvy', a play of feminine half-rhymes: 'auction / station / constitution / contagion / population / ocean / watchmen / fortifications / faction'. His only obtrusive concession to etymology is the word 'swishingly' in the penultimate line, 'The English swishingly they'll have laid low', which hints at the Irish *speal* or scythe underlying *spailpín*. As Muldoon himself puts it, 'it's a distortion that, like a funhouse mirror, is meant to include some clarification – in this case, on the use of the scythe as a weapon.'

When the Pie Was Opened is dedicated to the memory of Robert Fagles (1933-2008), whose muscular translations from Classical Greek will be well known to any reader of Penguin's excellent *Three Theban Plays* or the *Oresteia*. Muldoon includes a single poem from the Modern Greek of Kostis Palamas (1859-1943), who wrote, among other things, the words to the Olympic Hymn. In 'Gypsies', a section taken from Palamas's 'The Twelve Words of the Gypsy', he sets up a dizzying rhythm which is almost the rhythm of the trapeze:

tinkers who blow on their fire
as if fire

were the source of their power, then those whose wares
are smithy-smitches soldered to airs –

the gypsies who, as they've swung
from one land to the next, have lost their native tongue

and now switch languages as often as they switch
the switch they cut from the ditch,

> stealing words from all arts and parts
> and hitching them to their own words as to their carts
>
> they hitch stolen horses...

The swift, hypnotic rhythm is established not merely by the more obvious repetitions (switch/ditch/hitch, arts/parts/carts), though the morph of meaning in 'switch' is itself delightful, but by the embedded alliteration, half-rhyme and assonance which together animate the piece and give it its elasticity (fire/power/their/wares/airs, swung/one/tongue, next/native/now, etc.). 'Stealing' is a classic Muldoon pun harking back to 'smithy'. Notice, again, the importance of the vowel sounds in the following progression, from Ovid's 'Amores 1.5' : 'a half-slumber, / the shutter half-open, sunlight slanting through the slats / as it slants through a stand of timber', which freely renders the play of 'c', 'q', 'l', 'f' and 's' in the original: 'clausa fenestrae, / quale fere silvae lumen habere solent, / qualia sublucent fugiente crepuscula...'.

Amores is an erotic reverie, playful in Muldoon's characteristic 'Sam Spade' argot made famous in poems such as 'Immram': 'Right on cue, Corinna appeared, her dress undone'. Muldoon also has a lot of fun with Dafydd ap Gwilym's 'Y Gal', a mischievous, mock-accusatory harangue against the Welsh poet's own penis. Muldoon in his introduction takes it 'as my cue to meditate on some aspects of the testicles', presumably in his own poem 'Balls'. His translation of Gwilym's poem as 'The Cock', although inventive and suitably light in tone, is the occasion of an accumulation of some rather puerile puns, the kind of wordplay that might, one suspects, have made an adolescent Joyce snigger:

> You are a trouser-problem personified,
> suede-necked, gander-glide,
> congenital liar, pod from which indecency has sprung,
> nail on which injunctions are hung.
>
> Now you've once more been brought to book
> you should bow your head, you children's dibbling-hook.
> It's so hard to keep you in check,
> you pathetic little pecker-peck.
> Your master will stand in the dock because of you,
> because you're rotten through-and-through.

But this is not to detract from the chapbook as a whole, whose range and verbal opulence belies the nine bare poems of which it it consists.

Notes on Contributors

Joseph Allen's first collection is *Landscaping* (Flambard / Black Mountain, 2005); a pamphlet, *Night Patrol*, was published by Lapwing in 2001; his second collection, *Reading the Past*, is forthcoming from Lagan Press.

Peter Bakowski has had stints as writer-in-residence at the B R Whiting Library in Rome, the Cité Internationale des Arts in Paris, the Hobart Writer's Cottage in Battery Point, Tasmania, and elsewhere. He has facilitated poetry readings and workshops in schools, universities and to writing groups in Europe, Asia and throughout Australia.

Martin Bennett lives in Rome where he teaches and proof-reads at the University of Tor Vergata. Previous poems have appeared in *Poetry Ireland Review*, *Cyphers*, *Stand*, *Modern Poetry in Translation*, and elsewhere.

Pat Boran was born in Portlaoise in 1963 and has long since lived in Dublin. His latest publication is *New and Selected Poems* (Dedalus Press, 2007). A member of Aosdána, he received the 2008 Lawrence O'Shaughnessy Award for Poetry from the University of St Thomas Centre for Irish Studies, St Paul, Minnesota.

David Butler is a lecturer in the Humanities at Carlow College. His translations of Fernando Pessoa were published by Dedalus Press in 2004, and his novel *The Last European* was published in 2005.

Anthony Caleshu's first book of poems, *The Siege of the Body and a Brief Respite*, came out in 2004 from Salt Publishing; selections from the book were republished in *The New Irish Poets* (Bloodaxe Books) and *The Forward Book of Poetry 2005* (Faber and Faber). He is currently lecturer in English and Creative Writing at the University of Plymouth, SW England.

Louise C Callaghan has published two collections of poetry with Salmon Poetry: *The Puzzle-Heart* (1999) and *Remember the Birds* (2005). She edited and introduced an anthology of memory poems called *Forgotten Light* (A&A Farmar, 2003). In 2007 she completed a M.Litt in Creative Writing at St Andrews University, Scotland.

Mary Rose Callan's two collections of poetry are *The Mermaid's Head* (2001) and *Footfalls of Snow* (2005), both published by Bradshaw Books. Her work is included in a recent anthology of new Irish and Canadian poetry, *The Echoing Years*, and in *Thornfield*, an anthology of poems by the Thornfield Poets. A collection, *Learning to Swim*, is forthcoming from Bradshaw Books.

Patrick Carrington is the author of *Hard Blessings* (MSR Publishing, 2008), *Thirst* (Codhill, 2007), and *Rise, Fall and Acceptance* (MSR Publishing, 2006), and is the recipient of the 2008 Matt Clark Prize in poetry. His poetry has appeared in journals on both sides of the Atlantic. He teaches creative writing in New Jersey and is poetry editor of the journal *Mannequin Envy*.

Michael Coady's most recent publications from Gallery Press are *All Souls* and *One Another*, both books integrating poetry, prose and photographs. He is a member of Aosdána and lives in Carrick on Suir.

Colette Connor was born in Dublin. Her work has been published in *Poetry Ireland Review*, *The Cork Literary Review*, *Cyphers* and *Chapman*. She completed the M.Phil in Creative Writing at The Oscar Wilde Centre, Trinity College Dublin, in 2007.

Marie Coveney has exhibited for many years as a painter, winning the Éigse John J Duggan Painting Award in 2003. Her poem 'Our Time' won the American-Ireland Fund Single Poem Competition at the Listowel Literary Festival this year, and she will be published in the next issue of *THE SHOp*.

Ted Deppe directs Stonecoast in Ireland. Salmon Poetry published *Cape Clear: New and Selected Poems* in 2002, and Tupelo Press will bring out *Orpheus on the Red Line* in 2009.

Oliver Dunne has contributed illustrations to *Hot Press* and *The Sunday Independent* in the Republic of Ireland, and to *Punch* magazine / website in England. His poems have appeared in the anthologies *Lifelines 2* (TownHouse, 1994), *Human Rights Have No Borders: Voices of Irish Poets* (Marino, 1998) and *New and Collected Lifelines* (TownHouse, 2006).

Kristiina Ehin's *The Drums of Silence* (Oleander Press, 2007), a volume of her selected poems translated from her native Estonian, was awarded the Poetry Society Corneliu M Popescu Prize for European Poetry in Translation. Coiscéim will publish a new selection of her poems in a trilingual edition – Estonian with English and Irish translations.

Josh Ekroy has published in *Ragged Raven's* seventh and ninth anthologies of poetry in 2005 and 2007. He is the 2006 winner of the Strokestown Satirical Poetry Competition.

Luciano Erba was born in Milan in 1922. He is the author of numerous collections of poetry all brought together in *Poesie 1951-2001* (Mondadori, 2002), along with various translations, a short story collection, and a book of literary criticism. He has received most of Italy's major poetry awards including a Viareggio (1980), a Librex-Montale (1989) and a Pasolini (2005).

Pauline Gillan is an artist and a retired art teacher. 'Who Cares?', in this issue of *Poetry Ireland Review,* is her first published poem.

Jason Gray is the author of two chapbooks, *How to Paint the Savior Dead* (Kent State UP, 2007), winner of the Wick Chapbook Award, and *Adam & Eve Go to the Zoo* (Dream Horse, 2003). His poems have appeared in *Poetry, The American Poetry Review, The Prague Revue,* and elsewhere. He currently co-edits the online poetry journal *Unsplendid.*

Richard W Halperin is widely published in journals and anthologies in Ireland, the UK, mainland Europe and Canada. He conceived and edited the UNESCO booklet *Reading and Writing Poetry* (Paris, 2005) to stimulate enthusiasm for poetry teaching in secondary schools worldwide.

Noël Hanlon, from Portland Oregon, has had poems published in *The Texas Observer* and is on the board of the Soapstone Residency retreat for women writers.

Michael Heffernan's eighth book of poems, and his third published in Ireland, is *The Odor of Sanctity* from Salmon Poetry (2008). He lives in Fayetteville, Arkansas, where he has taught for the past twenty-two years at the University of Arkansas.

Fred Johnston founded Galway's Cúirt literary festival in 1986. A poet, novelist and short story writer, his most recent poetry collection is *The Oracle Room* (Cinnamon Press, 2007).

Maria Johnston is a part-time lecturer in Trinity College Dublin and Mater Dei Institute of Education. *High Pop: The Irish Times Column of Stewart Parker,* which she co-edited with Gerald Dawe, will be published by Lagan Press later this year.

Benjamin Keatinge is Head of English at the South East European University, Macedonia. He holds a doctorate on Samuel Beckett from Trinity College Dublin. His research interests include Beckett, Irish Modernism and contemporary Irish poetry, and he is currently co-editing a volume of critical essays on Brian Coffey, forthcoming from Irish Academic Press.

Alan Kellermann is working towards a Ph.D. at Swansea University in Swansea, Wales, where he is also poetry editor for the *Swansea Review.* His work has most recently appeared in *Planet* and *The Seventh Quarry.*

Kevin Kiely's most recent poetry collection is *Breakfast with Sylvia* (Lapwing Press, 2005). He has completed an authorised biography of Francis Stuart, *Francis Stuart: Artist and Outcast* (The Liffey Press, 2007), and is currently Fulbright Scholar in Residence at Boise State University, Idaho.

Ilmar Lehtpere is the translator of Kristiina Ehin's *The Drums of Silence* (Oleander Press, 2007), awarded the Poetry Society Corneliu M Popescu Prize for European Poetry in Translation.

Angela Long is a Canadian who has spent many years abroad. Her work has been published in various Canadian publications including *The Toronto Star*, *Prairie Fire* and *Arc*.

Catherine Phil MacCarthy's most recent poetry collection is *Suntrap* (Blackstaff Press, 2007). She is a former editor of *Poetry Ireland Review*.

Tom Mac Intyre was born and lives in Cavan. Recent publications include *ABC: New Poems* (2006) and a collection of short stories, *Find the Lady* (2008), both from New Island Books.

Michael McCarthy grew up in West Cork and lives in Yorkshire. A previous winner of the Patrick Kavanagh Award, his most recent publication is *Cold Hill Pond* from The Poetry Business.

Thomas McCarthy is an Irish poet, novelist and critic. He has published seven collections of poetry with Anvil Press, including *The Sorrow Garden*, *The Lost Province*, *Mr Dineen's Careful Parade* and *Merchant Prince*. He is also the author of two novels: *Without Power* and *Asya and Christine*.

Terry McDonagh's poetry collections include *Cill Aodáin & Nowhere Else* (Blaupause Books, 2008), with artwork by Sally McKenna, and *Boxes* (Blaupause Books, 2006) a collection for children.

Iggy McGovern's first collection, *The King of Suburbia* (Dedalus Press, 2005), received the inaugural Glen Dimplex New Writers Award for Poetry.

David McLoghlin received an Arts Council's Bursary in 2006 to allow him to dedicate almost a year to writing full time. In November 2007 he completed a memoir (*The Travelled Child*) about the Irish experience of emigration, writtenfrom a child's perspective. Most recently he was selected to participate in Poetry Ireland's 'Introductions' series of readings for 2008.

Cian Macken's poems have appeared in the anthology *Full Colour Sound, Ropes* and elsewhere. He is currently a student on the MA in Writing at NUI Galway.

Patrick Maddock is a former Hennessy Poetry Winner and was a runner-up in the Strokestown Poetry Festival's Political Poem section. His poems have appeared in various poetry magazines.

Máighréad Medbh, well known for her poetry performances, has published three collections of poetry and an audio CD. Her most recent collection is *Split*, published in *Divas!* (Arlen House, 2003). Another collection, *When the Air Inhales You*, will be published in November 2008.

Geraldine Mitchell lives near Louisburgh, Co Mayo, after many years in France, Algeria and Spain. She has written a biography and two novels for young people and is currently working on her first collection of poems.

Alan Jude Moore was twice short-listed for the New Irish Writing / Hennessy Literary Award for fiction. His first collection of poetry, *Black State Cars*, was published by Salmon Poetry in 2004. A second collection, *Lost Republics*, was published this year, also from Salmon Poetry.

Aidan Murphy was born in Cork in 1952 and now lives in Dublin. He has published six collections of poetry, including last year's *Neon Baby: Selected Poems* published by New Island Books.

Ainín Ní Bhroin previously published short fiction in *Cyphers* and in *Facing White*, an anthology of fiction and poetry by students from the M.Phil in Creative Writing at Trinity College Dublin.

Jean O'Brien is this year's recipient of the Fish International Poetry Award. Her previous collection, *Dangerous Dresses,* was published by Bradshaw Books in 2005, and her next, *As We Live It*, is due from Salmon Poetry in 2009. She currently teaches creative writing at the Irish Writers' Centre and for various County Councils.

Proinsias Ó Drisceoil is the author of *Seán Ó Dálaigh: Éigse agus Iomarbhá* (Cork University Press, 2007) and joint author of *Foclóir Litríochta agus Critice* (An Coisce Téarmaíochta, 2007). The latter is an English-Irish / Irish-English dictionary of literary terminology.

Rugadh **Simon Ó Faoláin** i mBaile Átha Cliath agus tógadh é don gcuid is mó i bParóiste Mhárthain in Iarthar Dhuibhneach. Is seandálaí gairmiúil é. Tá roinnt mhaith dá chuid fhoilsithe in irisí éagsúla, *Feasta*, *An Guth* agus *Cyphers* ina measc. Roinnt duaiseanna filíochta buaite aige, go h-áirithe Duais Cholm Cille 2008. Bhí a chéad chnuasach, *Anam Mhadra* choimisiúnaithe ag Bhord na Leabhar Gaeilge agus d'fhoilsigh Coiscéim é mí Lúnasa i mbliana.

Colette Olney has been published in *Cyphers* and *The Irish Times*, and read for Poetry Ireland's 'Introductions' series in 2007.

Michael O'Loughlin is currently Writer Fellow in Trinity College Dublin. His most recent collection is *Another Nation: New and Selected Poems*.

Peter Pegnall's most recent collections of poetry are *Through the Rock* (Blackwater Press, 2000) and *Foul Papers* (Lapwing Publications, 2006).

Anzhelina Polonskaya was born in Malakhovka, Russia. She published her first collection of poetry *My Heavenly Torch* in 1993. In 2004 an English-language collection, entitled *A Voice*, appeared in the 'Writings from an Unbound Europe' series at Northwestern University Press. This book was shortlisted for the 2005 Corneliu M Popescu Prize for European Poetry in Translation.

Ian Pople has taught English in the Sudan, Greece and Saudi Arabia, and is currently teaching at the University of Manchester. His first collection, *The Glass Enclosure* (Arc, 1996), was a Poetry Book Society Recommendation.

Susan Rich is the author of *Cures Include Travel* and a winner of the PEN USA Poetry Award and the Peace Corps Writers Award for T*he Cartographer's Tongue / Poems of the World*. Her work has appeared recently in *The Gettysburg Review*, *Notre Dame Review*, *New England Review* and *Poetry International*.

Peter Robinson published *The Look of Goodbye: Poems 2001–2006* (Shearsman) earlier in 2008. He was awarded this year's John Florio Prize for *The Greener Meadow: Selected Poems of Luciano Erba* (Princeton University Press, 2007). He is a Professor of English and American Literature at the University of Reading.

Mark Roper's collections include *The Hen Ark* (Peterloo/ Salmon Poetry, 1990), which won the 1992 Aldeburgh Prize for best first collection; *Catching The Light* (Peterloo/ Lagan Press, 1997) and *Whereabouts* (Peterloo/ Abbey Press, 2005). A *New and Selected Poems* is forthcoming from Dedalus Press.

Gabriel Rosenstock is a poet, haikuist and translator. Recent titles include his selected haiku in Irish *Géaga Trí Thine* (Comhar), the bilingual volume of poems *Bliain an Bhandé / Year of the Goddess* (Dedalus Press) and the anthology of sacred poetry *Guthanna Beannaithe an Domhain* (Coiscéim).

Damian Smyth's first collection, *Downpatrick Races*, was published by Lagan Press in 2000, and a play, *Soldiers of the Queen*, was produced at the Belfast Festival in 2002. *Market Street*, his third collection, is forthcoming this year. He is Literature Officer with the Arts Council of Northern Ireland.

Gerard Smyth has published six collections of poetry, the most recent of which are *A New Tenancy* (Dedalus Press, 2004) and *The Mirror Tent* (Dedalus Press, 2007).

Toon Tellegen, born in 1941, is one of Holland's best-known poets, with a long list of awards to his name. He is also a prolific children's book writer and novelist. Later this year Shoestring Press will publish a collection of his poetry in English translation, *About love and nothing else*.

Gráinne Tobin's collection *Banjaxed* was published in 2002 by Summer Palace Press. Her poems have been published in *Cyphers*, *Fortnight*, *Poetry Ireland Review*, and elsewhere.

Andrew Wachtel is Bertha and Max Dressler Professor in the Humanities at Northwestern University, Evanson, Illinois. He is the translator of Anzhelina Polonskaya's *A Voice: Selected Poems* (Northwestern University Press, 2004).

Judith Wilkinson is a British poet and bilingual translator. Her poems have been published in *The Literary Review*, *The Manhattan Review*, *PN Review*, *Poetry London*, and elsewhere. In 2007 she was runner-up for the David Reid Translation Prize. A collection of translations of the poetry of Toon Tellegen, *About love and about nothing else*, will be published by Shoestring Press later this year.

Macdara Woods has published 16 books plus CDs and other collaborations. His latest poetry publication is '15 Contacts' written in conjunction with Mayo County Council and the Percent for Art scheme. He is a member of Aosdána.

Previous Editors of *Poetry Ireland Review*

John Jordan 1–8	Spring 1981–Autumn 1983
Thomas McCarthy 9–12	Winter 1983–Winter 1984
Conleth Ellis and Rita E Kelly 13	Spring 1985
Terence Brown 14–17	Autumn 1985–Autumn1986
Ciaran Cosgrove 18–19	Spring 1987
Dennis O'Driscoll 20–21	Autumn 1987–Spring 1988
John Ennis and Rory Brennan 22–23	Summer 1988
John Ennis 24–25	Winter 1988–Spring 1989
Micheal O'Siadhail 26–29	Summer 1989–Summer1990
Máire Mhac an tSaoi 30–33	Autumn 1990–Winter 1991
Peter Denman 34–37	Spring 1992–Winter 1992
Pat Boran 38	Summer 1993
Seán Ó Cearnaigh 39	Autumn 1993
Pat Boran 40–42	Winter 1993–Summer 1994
Chris Agee 43–44	Autumn/Winter 1994
Moya Cannon 45–48	Spring 1995–Winter 1995
Liam Ó Muirthile 49	Spring 1996
Michael Longley 50	Summer 1996
Liam Ó Muirthile 51–52	Autumn 1996–Spring 1997
Frank Ormsby 53–56	Summer 1997–Spring 1998
Catherine Phil MacCarthy 57–60	Summer 1998–Spring 1999
Mark Roper 61–64	Summer 1999– Spring 2000
Biddy Jenkinson 65–68	Summer 2000–Spring 2001
Maurice Harmon 69–72	Summer 2001–Spring 2002
Michael Smith 73–75	Summer 2002–Winter 2002/3
Eva Bourke 76	Spring/Summer 2003
Peter Sirr 77–91	Autumn 2003 / October 2007

What do *you* see?

Poetry Ireland Review